Dear Jill 8-17-2010

Interracial Intimacies
An Examination of Powerful Men and Their Relationships across the Color Line

Earl Smith
WAKE FOREST UNIVERSITY

Angela J. Hattery
WAKE FOREST UNIVERSITY

CAROLINA ACADEMIC PRESS
Durham, North Carolina

Library of Congress Cataloging-in-Publication Data

Smith, Earl, 1946-
Interracial intimacies : an examination of powerful men and
their relationships across the color line / Earl Smith and Angela
Hattery.
    p. cm.
Includes index.
ISBN 978-1-59460-496-6 (alk. paper)
1. Race relations--United States--History. 2. Group identity--
United States--History. I. Hattery, Angela. II. Title.
HT1507.S65 2009
305.800973--dc22
                                        2009017894

CAROLINA ACADEMIC PRESS
700 Kent Street
Durham, North Carolina 27701
Telephone (919) 489-7486
Fax (919) 493-5668
www.cap-press.com

Interracial Intimacies

To Travis and Emma, as always.
You make the joys of parenting outweigh the struggles.
—Mom

To Earl:
This book was truly fun. I enjoyed learning about the
lives of these fascinating people, reading to you out loud
some of the most outrageous quotes in their biographies
and autobiographies, and struggling to find a way to
make sense of it all. I can't imagine it any other way.
—Angie

To Angie:
Years ago, as a new assistant professor at Washington
State University, I was told that I should do this book.
I said, "no." Instead I worked with several graduate
students researching their theses and dissertations on
topics all associated with interracial relationships.
The topic, the stories, the injustices stayed with me all
this time; but I never actually touched it.
It took our discussions and insights to finally
intellectually address the issues herein. And it was fun.
As always, THANK YOU!
—Earl

Contents

Acknowledgments

This book began as an interest in what we, as outsiders, perceived as the complex and often contradictory lives led by southern men of power, men like Thomas Jefferson and Strom Thurmond, who engaged in racist practices while simultaneously having long-standing, intimate relationships with African American women. Intrigued by the cognitive dissonance inherent in these practices, we set out to learn as much as we could about Jefferson and Thomas. As we began to more fully explore their lives, among other things we learned that these men, their relationships, and their lives are much more complex than we first anticipated. We are grateful to all the other scholars and biographers who provided the "data" that we used to write this book.

Second, we are grateful to our historian colleagues, who, upon hearing about the project, pointed us toward lesser-known individuals whose relationships were equally compelling. In particular we are grateful to Professor Paul Escott, Reynolds Professor of History at Wake Forest University, who not only offered us insight on Thomas Jefferson but introduced us to Richard Mentor Thomas, a figure neither of us had heard of previously.

We acknowledge the background biographical research that Travis Mathew Hattery Freetly did—for pay—especially his contributions to the chapters on Mildred and Richard Loving, William Cohen and Janet Langhart Cohen, and Strom Thurmond.

We are grateful for the insight and support of our editors at Carolina Academic Press, especially Beth Hall.

Finally, we are grateful for the opportunity once again to work with each other on a project that is not only intellectually interesting but provided many occasions for surprise, astonishment and laughter.

Interracial Intimacies

Chapter One

Introduction

As the good book says, "Each shall seek his own kind."
In other words a bird may love a fish, but where would
they build a home together?

Tevye, *Fiddler on the Roof*

In this book we examine several issues about interracial intimate relationships. Our focus is on highly visible individuals—White and
African American—many of whom openly oppose/opposed such
relationships. In some instances, these same individuals have par-
ticipated in acts blocking such relationships (e.g., the passage of a
bill, disowning offspring, openly supporting the continuance of
segregated schools, etc.), while at the same time they were involved
in intimate, interracial relationships themselves.

We wonder how White men who believe that people of African
American descent are less than fully human, or who campaigned
on the platform of Jim Crow segregation, reconciled these beliefs
alongside their long-term, intimate relationships with African American women. Furthermore, we explore these issues alongside our
firmly held belief, as we did in a recent publication on social stratification in the South, that the human separation or in sociological terminology, social segregation, of people based on their race
is illogical (Hattery and Smith 2007; Merton 1948).

It seems unbelievable that throughout most of U.S. history, essential American institutions, such as municipalities, cities, school
districts, the American Red Cross, movie theatres, churches, professional baseball teams, restaurants, and lending institutions like
banks, all mandated—*de jure* or *de facto*—American people of
different ethnicities to be separated, no matter the financial or

human cost. The financial costs alone of building, maintaining, and operating separate schools, hospitals, blood banks, churches, separate everything are remarkable.

These barriers existed everywhere. This is especially true of neighborhoods (Correa 2001; Logan, Zhang, and Alba 2002; Stearns and Logan 1986) but also in places one would never suspect. For example, at a time when African American men were volunteering for war duty during World War I and World War II, the growing African American middle class could not escape Jim Crow on the highways and in the national parks of America. In a fascinating research paper entitled "The Open Road: Automobility and Racial Uplift in the Inter War Years," Franz (2001: 13–14) notes that

> [W]hite auto camp owners routinely refused black travelers upon arrival ... even the National Parks, the epitome of the open road movement for many white Americans, perpetuated racial discrimination.

While this type of segregation seems rare, it was not. In other quarters, for example, we find similar barriers to equality. The American Red Cross had deep difficulties in setting up non-discriminatory blood donor policies in both civilian hospitalities and the Army and Navy after Pearl Harbor (Parks 1973). According to Parks (1973: 148)

> On 27 December 1941, the *Pittsburg Courier* announced that both the Army and Navy were unwilling to authorize the American Red Cross to accept blood from Negro donors.

Legal scholar Randall Kennedy (Kennedy 2003) discusses the complex, troubling life of Ruby Henley, a White female and mother of Jacqueline Henley, and lays bear the illogical nature of social segregation and how it is found in some of the most unexpected places. Kennedy described Jacqueline's fate (2003: 3):

> Jacqueline Henley's aunt turned her niece over to the custody of the New Orleans department of Welfare on October 1, 1952, because she was becoming darker by the day and some of the neighbors had complained that

"the child possibly was a nigger." Jacqueline was not yet two years old.

How "becoming darker" is a condition for abandonment needs to be explained — it is absurd, even in the context of the Jim Crow South, and even moreso for the yet-to-be two-year-old Jacqueline, whom Kennedy describes.

Social segregation critically shaped intimate relationships, including many which we detail in this book. First and foremost, social segregation shapes the "pool" from which we each draw our intimate partners. Regardless of one's attitudes toward interracial relationships, one has to have opportunities to meet and interact with people of other racial/ethnic groups in order for the possibility of an interracial relationship to even exist. Secondly, for many of the people we profile in this book, social segregation and laws against interracial marriage stood as significant barriers for a loving relationship to become a stable, permanent, publicly recognized relationship.[1] Thus, the history and pattern of social segregation throughout U.S. history was critical to the development of the relationships we analyzed in the book.

This book is about the inconsistencies, "cultural contradictions" (Smith and Hattery 2009), in interracial relationships mainly in the lives and life chances of prominent men (and some women) who profess the *wrongs* to be found in so-called "race-mixing" while simultaneously they, themselves, were intimately involved with a man or woman of another race. Indeed we will argue that in order to deal with the contradictions in their own lives, several of the people we profile in this book actually contributed to the ideologies and laws of the United States in ways that negatively impacted the lives of those who were attempting to create loving, stable in a time or place in which interracial relationships were not only abhorred but illegal.[2]

---

1. This volume only reports on intimate relationships in heterosexual relationships. See our companion volume, *Interracial Relationships in the 21st Century* for research on homosexual/lesbian interracial relationships.

2. Without delving into the complex and controversial arguments about race, we use the term throughout in its colloquial sense in 21st century America.

Racial Identity and the "One Drop Rule"

Though focused on the intimate relationships between adult men and women across the racial divide, this book, by necessity, must address the issue of racial identity, for only when racial identities are non-overlapping and mutually exclusive can there be a boundary that must be protected and subsequently crossed. Historically in the United States, the "rule" that prevailed in the establishment of racial identity was the "one drop rule" (Johnston 1970). Quite simply, one drop of "Black blood" meant that one was "Black." The one drop rule was the fundamental rule for establishing racial identity.

Like so many laws and social issues in the U.S., the anti-miscegenation laws were applied very differently based on the race, gender, and social class of the parties involved. For example, as noted by Angela Davis, African American men were lynched for alleging having sexual relations with White women, even when the relations were consensual.[3] Yet, it is widely known that throughout U.S. social history, White men had consensual and non-consensual sexual relations with African American women and were not penalized for these actions — even when they were non-consensual. These violations of the anti-miscegenation laws were not only overlooked or ignored; in many cases they were actually sanctioned.[4] It is common knowledge now, as it was then, that White slave owners raped their African American female slaves as a strategy for increasing their property. Children born to these slave women were, by definition, identified as "Black," they were the

---

3. In some cases, such as Emmitt Till, African American men were lynched for as little as looking at or talking to White women. See especially Patterson, Orlando. 1999. *Rituals of Blood: Consequences of Slavery in Two American Centuries.* New York: Civitas. Angela Davis, "Rape, Racism and the Myth of the Black Rapist" in *Women, Race, and Class.* New York: Vintage Books, 1983.

4. The twists and turns of these violations are found in the long-neglected Ph.D. dissertation (1937) and now a book by Johnson, James Hugo. 1970. *Race Relations in Virginia and Miscegenation in the South.* Amherst, MA: The University of Massachusetts Press.

property of the slave master, and they lived out their lives in slavery. In some cases, White male slave owners had long-standing sexual relationships with one or more Black female slaves. We will explore some examples of this among well-known slave owners and public figures such as George Washington, Thomas Jefferson, and Richard Mentor Johnson.

However, the issue is far more complex than the racial identity of the children of these couplings. As Williamson (Williamson [1980] 1995) addresses, these sexual liaisons across the color boundary created a third race of people who populated the young United States: mulattos. Based on his analysis of the 1850 census, as much as 10 percent of the "Black" population and 2 percent of the overall U.S. population was categorized as "mulatto" (Williamson [1980] 1995). Not only is this fascinating, but it raises the issue of the racial identity of "mulattos." Though commonly referred to by this term (in Chapter Five we examine the life of Vice-President Richard Johnson, who "married" a mulatto woman), because of the intractability of the one-drop rule and the ideology of the immutability and biological determinism of race and racial identity, "mulattos" were still categorized by the census and for the purposes of segregation, legal matters, contracts, and civil rights as "Black."

It seems a simple question, yet one that is rarely asked: Why are all "mulattos" "Black" and none of them "White?" Recall that Williamson's (Williamson [1980] 1995) research on the 1850 census reveals the percentage of "Blacks" who are mulatto. Never does the census report the percentage of "Whites" who are mulatto.

Omi and Winant offer some insight, citing the case of Susie Guillory Phipps (1986: 53):

> In 1982–83, Susie Guillory Phipps unsuccessfully sued the Louisiana Bureau of Vital Records to change her racial classification from Black to White. The descendent of an 18th century White planter and a Black slave, Phipps was designated as "Black" on her birth certificate in accordance with a 1970 state law which declared anyone with at least 1/32nd "Negro blood" to be Black ... Phipps attorney, Brian Begue, argued that ... the 1/32nd

designation was inaccurate. He called on a retired Tulane University professor who cited research indicating that most Louisiana whites have a least 1/20th "Negro" ancestry.

As we are fond of saying, how come a White woman can have a "Black" baby—or mulatto—but a Black woman can't have a White baby—though she can and indeed many Black women did have mulatto babies? This example illustrates clearly that the racial category of "White" is fixed, whereas that racial category of "Black" is fluid and can be expanded to "absorb" people who are mixed-race or have what we now refer to as multiracial heritage.

When we analyze race and interracial relationships using a biological or genetic framework, this seems absurd. For example, we might ask of Vice-President Richard Johnson, whose interracial relationship with his wife, the mulatto Julia Chinn, produced daughters who had all of the rights that Whites possessed—they were educated, they legally married White men, and they inherited property—how did they become "White," when children of a similar union, that between Thomas Jefferson and Sally Hemings, also a mulatto, did not become "White" until after Jefferson's death? Furthermore, think of the absurdity that the children of Sally Hemings and Thomas Jefferson were (1) born "Black", (2) categorized as "mulatto" in the special census of 1833 that attempted to identify people of African descent who wished to be returned to Africa, and (3) became "White" when they moved to Ohio and changed their names and claimed this racial identity (Gordon-Reed 2008).

Racial identity, as Omi and Winant (1986), Bonilla-Silva (2001) and others point out, is a matter of power. The children of Jefferson, Johnson, Thurmond and others adopted different racial identities and statuses as a result of social circumstances and power, not biology or genetics.

Thus, though this book examines interracial couplings, specifically those between "Whites" and "Blacks," we focus specifically on the role that power plays in shaping the negotiation of intimate relationships, family forms, racial identity, hegemonic ideology and public policy among public figures who not only contributed to the public discourses on race and interracial unions, but also contributed to the racial ideologies that gained hegemony and dominated Americans' beliefs about race and the laws and public policies that established second class citizenship for those identified as "Black."

We begin the book with a discussion of Mildred and Richard Loving, because it is their relationship that ultimately brings the challenge to the U.S. Supreme Court and leads to the toppling of anti-miscegenation laws. We follow this chapter with a discussion of Thomas Jefferson, because he is perhaps the most "famous" of the people whose lives we examine, and because his relationship across the color line was highly contested into the beginning of the 21st century. The chapters follow more or less in chronological order after that, though we end the book with the chapter on Strom Thurmond for many of the same reasons we began with Jefferson.

Chapter Two

Mildred and Richard Loving: The Case That Changed American Interracial Marriage Laws

Scholars, especially historians of the Southern United States, have always argued that interracial relationships, especially Black/White relationships (but also Native and White), have been a part of these United States of America since the founding of the Union, if not before. (Aptheker 1951–1994; Berry 1994; Faragher 1994;[1] Foner 2002)

Interracial unions and the norms and laws that govern them are central to the individual cases we examine in this book. Interracial unions involving the founding fathers of the United States of America—George Washington and Thomas Jefferson—were simply treated as a private matter. And, as we noted in the introduction, it is a well-established fact that plantation owners had a variety of sexual liaisons with their female slaves ranging from the non-consensual to the "one night stand" to full blown relationships that were effectively common law marriages.

---

1. Turner is remembered for his "Frontier Thesis," which he first published July 12, 1893, in a paper read in Chicago to the American Historical Association during the Chicago World's Fair. In it, he stated that the spirit and success of the United States is directly tied to the country's westward expansion. According to Turner, the forging of the unique and rugged American identity occurred at the juncture between the civilization of settlement and the savagery of wilderness. This produced a new type of citizen—one with the power to tame the wild and one upon whom the wild had conferred strength and individuality.

While we detail these "relationships" throughout the book, the "case" of Mildred and Richard Loving departs significantly from the other chapters in that it does not involve individuals who are public figures, living a public life, nor do either of them expound from some platform with some specific public discourse on race. Yet, to talk about interracial couplings in the United States and *not* talk about Mildred and Richard Loving would be remiss.[2] Because neither was a public figure, and their most public legacy is the legal case—based on their marriage—that rendered anti-miscegenation laws unconstitutional, there is a great deal written about the case, but very little written about the lives of Mildred and Richard Loving.

The 1967 case of *Loving v. Virginia*, heard by the Earl Warren court, ruled in favor of the Lovings, deeming the Racial Integrity Act of 1924 unconstitutional, and thus rendering all laws prohibiting interracial marriages unconstitutional and thus making interracial marriages legal *throughout* the United States. This case sprung from the marriage of Mildred Loving, an African American woman, and Richard Loving, a White man. The couple had fled Caroline County, Virginia, to get married, because Caroline County did not recognize or permit interracial marriages. Upon their return to Caroline County, they were charged with miscegenation.

Mildred and Richard both grew up in rural Virginia in a community called Central Point in Caroline County. Central Point, like many Southern towns in the Jim Crow South, was characterized as having two distinct sets of racial ideology: segregation was both law and custom, but there was a long history of interracial unions—in fact, Caroline County was known for having "many mulatto children that blended in with White children." (Staples 2008) Slave owners in Virginia, such as Thomas Jefferson, about whom we will write extensively in Chapter Three, were known to have illegitimate children with their slaves. (Staples 2008)

The 19th-century diarist Mary Boykin Chesnut could easily have been speaking of Caroline County planters when she wrote:

---

2. *Loving et Ux. v. Virginia*, Supreme Court of the United States, 388 U.S. 1 (June 12, 1967, Decided).

Like the patriarchs of old, our men live all in one house
with their wives and their concubines; and the mulattoes one sees in every family partly resemble the White
children. (Staples 2008)

Because of the norms and standards that were well established and
deeply entrenched in Central Point, there was not only a large bi-
racial population, but many Central Point residents who were legally
been categorized as "Black" under the one-drop rule, were able to
"pass" when they traveled or moved into communities outside of
Central Point. Former residents were able to attend all-White schools
and even serve in the all-White units of the segregated armed forces
during World War II. (Staples 2008) Furthermore,

The community developed a system for protecting the
racial identities of Central Pointers who moved away
and married into White families. When they took their
White relatives back with them to visit, their younger
brothers and sisters, who attended the colored school,
just stayed home. This was well known to the teachers
at the school, who apparently accepted the absences
without question. (Staples 2008)

Thus, the community in which Mildred and Richard were born
and raised, which had a long history and " ... made an art form of
evading Jim Crow restrictions on relationships ..." (Staples 2008)
was instrumental in shaping both Mildred and Richard's attitudes
toward interracial love and makes the only unusual part about their
story the fact that they were charged with a felony for marrying
outside of the state of Virginia.

The Lovings became friends during their childhood, although
Richard was six years Mildred's senior. They met when Mildred
was six years old and Richard was eleven years old. (*Economist*
2008) Once Mildred reached the legal age to marry—eighteen—
the two were wed in Washington, D.C., on July 2, 1958. An unexpected pregnancy is believed to have greatly influenced the couple's
decision. (*Economist* 2008; Walker 2008) The two were forced to
marry outside of Virginia because interracial marriages were still il-

legal in Virginia in 1958. They were in such a rush that they simply picked the minister's name out of the phone book. (*Economist* 2008; Stritof 2008)

A mere five weeks after their marriage, once they returned to Virginia, police awoke them in the middle of the night and arrested them for being married. According to *The Economist*, the problem was not that they were in bed together, but that they were married.

> She told the sheriff, "I'm his wife." And Mr. Loving, roused at last, pointed to the framed certificate above the bed [they had framed their marriage license and hung it above their bed]. "That's no good here," Sheriff Brooks said. Mrs. Loving had said the wrong thing. Had they just been going together, Black and White, no one would have cared much. But they had formalized their love, and had the paperwork. This meant that under Virginia law they were cohabiting "against the peace and dignity of the Commonwealth." It was a felony for Blacks and Whites to marry, and another felony to leave Virginia to do so. Fifteen other states had similar laws. The Lovings had to get up and go to jail. "The Lord made sparrows and robins, not to mix with one another," as Sheriff Brooks said later. (*Economist* 2008)

One might wonder how anyone even knew about their marriage and how the sheriff was "tipped off" that they had returned and were living as husband and wife in Central Point. Staples (2008) offers an explanation:

> The state officials who enforced segregation were clearly aware of what Central Point's residents were up to and tried to stop it. They circulated lists of families described as descendants of Black people. For a time, the state "corrected" birth certificates to note the "real" race of the bearer. It didn't change things much in Central Point.

The Lovings pleaded guilty to their charge with a minimum sentence of one year and a maximum of five; they were sentenced to one year in prison, but the sentence was suspended for twenty-five years as long as the Lovings never came back to Virginia together within those twenty-five years. "According to University of Georgia professor and family friend Robert Pratt, they got around it by riding back in separate cars and meeting up." (Walker, 2008) Frustrated, Mildred told her story to the Attorney General, Robert F. Kennedy, and attorney Bernard S. Cohen took their case. After a nine-year struggle, the Supreme Court unanimously ruled in the Lovings' favor. The remaining sixteen states that enforced interracial marriage laws were forced to abolish them. However, many laws remained on the books, especially in the Deep South, even if they could not be legally enforced; it was not until 2000, when Alabama finally removed their law from the books, that no more interracial marriage laws existed. (Stritof 2008)

The Lovings remained married until 1975, when a drunk driver killed Richard; he died at forty-one years of age. Mildred lived until 2008, when she died of pneumonia at the age of sixty eight. They had three children; Donald who died in 2000, Peggy and Sidney. To the day she died, Mildred remained quiet about her story, a fame she never necessarily wished for. She let others tell her story through books and articles, including a Showtime film *Mr. and Mrs. Loving*; although Mildred claims that, "The only part of it right was I had three children." (Walker 2008)

In honor of the couple's courage, every year on June 12th, interracial couples across America celebrate "Loving Day." And, it is the Supreme Court ruling that is named for them that enables interracial couples, including several profiled in this book, to enjoy the legal benefits and privileges of marriage today. We conclude this chapter with a speech by Mildred Loving given on the 40th anniversary of the U.S. Supreme Court decision that struck down all state prohibitions on interracial marriages.

Loving for All

By Mildred Loving *
Prepared for Delivery on June 12, 2007,
The 40th Anniversary of the *Loving vs. Virginia* Announcement

When my late husband, Richard, and I got married in Washington, DC in 1958, it wasn't to make a political statement or start a fight. We were in love, and we wanted to be married.

We didn't get married in Washington because we wanted to marry there. We did it there because the government wouldn't allow us to marry back home in Virginia where we grew up, where we met, where we fell in love, and where we wanted to be together and build our family. You see, I am a woman of color and Richard was white, and at that time people believed it was okay to keep us from marrying because of their ideas of who should marry whom.

When Richard and I came back to our home in Virginia, happily married, we had no intention of battling over the law. We made a commitment to each other in our love and lives, and now had the legal commitment, called marriage, to match. Isn't that what marriage is?

Not long after our wedding, we were awakened in the middle of the night in our own bedroom by deputy sheriffs and actually arrested for the "crime" of marrying the wrong kind of person. Our marriage certificate was hanging on the wall above the bed.

The state prosecuted Richard and me, and after we were found guilty, the judge declared: "Almighty God created the races white, black, yellow, malay and red, and he placed them on separate continents. And but for the interference with his arrangement there would be no cause for such marriages. The fact that he separated the races shows that he did not intend for the races to mix." He sentenced us to a year in prison, but offered to suspend the sentence if we left our home in Virginia for 25 years exile.

We left, and got a lawyer. Richard and I had to fight, but still were not fighting for a cause. We were fighting for our love.

Though it turned out we had to fight, happily Richard and I didn't have to fight alone. Thanks to groups like the ACLU and the NAACP Legal Defense & Education Fund, and so many good people around the country willing to speak up, we took our case for the freedom to marry all the way to the U.S. Supreme Court. And on June 12, 1967, the Supreme Court ruled unanimously that, "The freedom to marry has long been recognized as one of the vital personal rights essential to the orderly pursuit of happiness by free men," a "basic civil right."

My generation was bitterly divided over something that should have been so clear and right. The majority believed that what the judge said, that it was God's plan to keep people apart, and that government should discriminate against people in love. But I have lived long enough now to see big changes. The older generation's fears and prejudices have given way, and today's young people realize that if someone loves someone they have a right to marry.

Surrounded as I am now by wonderful children and grandchildren, not a day goes by that I don't think of Richard and our love, our right to marry, and how much it meant to me to have that freedom to marry the person precious to me, even if others thought he was the "wrong kind of person" for me to marry. I believe all Americans, no matter their race, no matter their sex, no matter their sexual orientation, should have that same freedom to marry. Gov-

ernment has no business imposing some people's religious beliefs over others. Especially if it denies people's civil rights.

I am still not a political person, but I am proud that Richard's and my name is on a court case that can help reinforce the love, the commitment, the fairness, and the family that so many people, black or white, young or old, gay or straight seek in life. I support the freedom to marry for all. That's what Loving, and loving, are all about.

Chapter Three

Thomas Jefferson: Father of Democracy and Racial Ideology

In this chapter, we explore the complex and often contradictory life of one of America's Founding Fathers and most influential figures—the third president of the United States, Thomas Jefferson.

Early Life

Thomas Jefferson was born April 13, 1743, in Albemarle County, Virginia. He was the son of Peter Jefferson and Jane Randolph. His father's family was among the first settlers in Virginia, and his mother's family was considered one of the most prestigious in the colony. The first biographer of Jefferson, B.L. Rayner, who published his biography just eight years after Jefferson's death, notes that Jefferson's father was charged with determining and drawing the boundary between Virginia and North Carolina, and was also commissioned to create the first "regular map" of Virginia. (Rayner 1834)

As part of the gentry class, Thomas Jefferson received a formal education beginning his studies in "English school at age five and Latin school at age nine." (Thomas Jefferson Encyclopedia) Jefferson spent seven years studying at the College of William and Mary in Williamsburg, Virginia. After this course of study, he had the appropriate education and credentials necessary to practice law. (Thomas Jefferson Encyclopedia)[1]

---

1. In the 1700s, American universities like William and Mary followed the British system of education wherein a student "read law" with a pro-

Professional Life

After practicing law for a brief period of time, Jefferson's life as a public figure truly began with his election to the Continental Conference in 1775. In 1776, he was tapped for what would perhaps be his greatest contribution to the new experiment in democracy: the drafting of the Declaration of Independence. Before taking national office, Jefferson served as the governor of Virginia from 1779–81. Jefferson was elected to Congress, representing Virginia, in 1783. He served as the first United States Secretary of State (1790–93), as Vice-President (1797–1801), and was elected as the third President of the United States in 1801; he served two terms in this capacity (1801–1809) before retiring from public service. Perhaps the most notable achievements of his first term were the purchase of the Louisiana Territory in 1803 and his support of the Lewis and Clark expedition. Finally, one of his greatest legacies was his work to found the University of Virginia, one of the top universities in the nation today, which opened in 1825, just a year before Jefferson died. (Thomas Jefferson Foundation)

Of all of the individuals whose lives are explored in this book, perhaps the person who wrote most extensively about race is Thomas Jefferson. He was a prolific author who had ample opportunity to reflect on the emerging country that was built on principles of democracy and equality; novel ideas for the late 18th century world in which Jefferson lived. Though most historians note the tremendous legacy of Thomas Jefferson, less attention is paid to the dissonance between Jefferson's principles and his practices.

As noted in our discussion of Jefferson's early life, he was born into a position of significant privilege. In an age when few Americans were formally educated, Jefferson studied for seven years and was ultimately "certified" to practice law. In an era in which many Americans scraped out a meager existence, Jefferson inherited tremendous property—including slaves—from both his father

---

fessor but was not granted a formal degree. (Thomas Jefferson Encyclopedia)

and father-in-law. He broke ground for Monticello when he was only 25 years old (having inherited the property at age 21 when his father died) and in 1774, at the tender age of 31, he inherited 11,000 acres of land and 135 slaves—among them, Sally Hemings—from his father-in-law, John Waylcs.

In addition to his privilege as an educated, landed man in the 18th century, Jefferson was a successful planter and slave owner. Though he is known around the world for his discourse on equality and human rights, it is important to contextualize his comments by considering them alongside his status as a slave owner and beneficiary of the slave economy of the rural southern United States; indeed, his home in rural Virginia placed him in the largest and longest slave-owning state in the United States. While many historians note that Jefferson did free some of his slaves, official records indicate that he freed only a handful and did not even include his lover Sally Hemings.

> Jefferson had a number of slaves who gained their freedom by various methods. He freed two slaves in his lifetime and five in his will. Three others ran away and were not pursued. All nine freed with Jefferson's consent were members of the Hemings family; the seven he officially freed were all skilled tradesmen. About 200 slaves were sold at estate sales after Jefferson's death. (Thomas Jefferson Encyclopedia)

We are not the first to note the apparent dissonance between Jefferson's beliefs on equality—as expressed in his writings—and his lived reality. Indeed, this matter is even addressed by the Thomas Jefferson Foundation. We quote their explanation in its entirety so the reader can see the ways in which an official organization like this attempts to address the obvious dissonance in Jefferson's life. (Note: emphasis is ours.)

> Thomas Jefferson was a consistent opponent of slavery throughout his life. He considered it contrary to the laws of nature that decreed that everyone had a right to personal liberty. He called the institution an "abom-

inable crime," a "moral depravity," a "hideous blot," and a "fatal stain" that deformed "what nature had bestowed on us of her fairest gifts."

Early in his political career Jefferson took actions that he hoped would end in slavery's abolition. He drafted the Virginia law of 1778 prohibiting the importation of enslaved Africans. In 1784, he proposed an ordinance banning slavery in the new territories of the Northwest. From the mid-1770s, he advocated a plan of gradual emancipation, by which all born into slavery after a certain date would be declared free.

As historian David Brion Davis noted, if Jefferson had died in 1785, he would be remembered as an antislavery hero, as "one of the first statesmen anywhere to advocate concrete measures for eradicating slavery." After that time, however, there came a "thundering silence." *Jefferson made no public statements on American slavery nor did he take any significant public action to change the course of his state or his nation.*

Countless articles and even entire books have been written trying to explain the contradictions between Jefferson's words and actions in regard to slavery. His views on race, which he first broadcast in his *Notes on the State of Virginia* in 1785, unquestionably affected his behavior. His belief in the inferiority of Blacks, coupled with their presumed resentment of their former owners, made their removal from the United States an integral part of Jefferson's emancipation scheme. These convictions were exacerbated by the bloody revolution in Haiti and an aborted rebellion of slaves and free Blacks in Virginia in 1800.

While slavery remained the law of the land, *Jefferson struggled to make ownership of humans compatible with the new ideas of the era of revolutions. By creating a moral*

*and social distance between himself and enslaved people,
by pushing them down the "scale of beings," he could consider himself as the "father" of "children" who needed his
protection.* As he wrote of slaves in 1814, "brought up from
their infancy without necessity for thought or forecast,
[they] are by their habits rendered as incapable as children of taking care of themselves." In the manner of
other paternalistic slaveholders, he thus saw himself as
the benevolent steward of the African Americans to
whom he was bound in a relation of mutual depen-
dency and obligation. By 1820, during the political crisis that resulted in the Missouri Compromise, Jefferson
had come to believe that the spread of slavery into the
west—its "diffusion"—would prove beneficial to the
slaves and hasten the end of the institution. The prospect
of a geographical line based on principle running across
the country, "like a fire bell in the night, awakened and
filled me with terror." He feared it could threaten the
union and lead to civil war. *As always, his primary concern was the stability of the nation he had helped to found.*
Almost forty years after Jefferson's death, slavery ended
by the bloodiest war in American history. (Thomas Jefferson Encyclopedia)

This long passage from the Thomas Jefferson Foundation is an attempt by an institution with a vested interest in promoting Jefferson's legacy to make sense of the apparent disconnect in Jefferson's
life. And, though much of the argument is quite compelling, we
argue that the suggestion that Jefferson's decision to become silent
on the issue of slavery because he feared a civil war—which of
course transpired anyway—while he simultaneously had a long-
term relationship with a slave he owned and with whom he fathered
children, is insufficient at best. Furthermore, we suggest that it is
similar to the path taken by Senator Strom Thurmond 150 years
later: Mr. Thurmond secretly installed his daughter at a local historically Black college so that he had access to her and could pay her
tuition, while he simultaneously ran for president on the segrega-

tionist platform. It seems clear that Thurmond, too, believed that an oppressive social institution was appropriate for the country despite the fact that it led to the oppression of his own daughter. We will return to this discussion in Chapter Nine.

There are, of course, critical differences between Jefferson and Thurmond; namely the fact that Jefferson wrote about equality, whereas Thurmond never claimed to adhere to an ideology of equality, and the men lived in different eras and took different approaches to dealing with the apparent contradictions between their beliefs about race and interracial relationships and the interracial relationships they carried on for decades. Chapter Nine is devoted in its entirety to a discussion of Thurmond's life.

In contrast to the Thomas Jefferson Foundation's interpretation of the apparent dissonance between Jefferson's rhetoric and his behavior, others who have studied this disconnect have not necessarily differed in the content of their argument, but have not been as forgiving of Jefferson's actions. (Okoye 1980)

As noted by the Thomas Jefferson Foundation, Jefferson engaged in rhetorical justifications that allowed him to make congruent his beliefs about equality—the very principle he felt the newly born United States was built on—and his decision to remain silent on the issue of slavery. In order to create compatibility between these seemingly divergent perspectives, Jefferson developed an ideology of race and human nature that incorporated a hierarchy of being that placed Whites at the top and those of African descent at the bottom.

> In general their existence appears to participate more of sensation than reflection.... [I]n memory they are equal to Whites, in reason much inferior.... [and]in imagination they are dull, tasteless, and anomalous.... I advance it therefore ... that the Blacks, whether originally a different race, or made distinct by time and circumstances, are inferior to Whites ... Will not a lover of natural history, then, one who views the gradations in all the animals with the eye of philosophy, excuse an effort to keep those in the department of Man (sic) as distinct as nature has formed them. (Jefferson 1787: 270)

According to Omi and Winant: "Such claims of species distinc-
tiveness among humans justified the inequitable allocation of political and social rights, while still upholding the doctrine of the
"rights of man." (1994: 64) And, given Jefferson's incredible power
to reach a wide audience, we can only infer the powerful influence
that his re-conceptualization of people of African descent as biologically inferior—developed as a justification for denying them
human and civil right—had on thinkers, teachers, politicians, and
religious leaders of the time.

Jefferson's beliefs about people of African descent were also expressed in his writings about interracial unions. According to Jefferson historian Bruce Fehn, Jefferson was also a miscegenist: "In
a letter to Edward Coles, Jefferson described slaves as 'children' and
interracial unions as producing what he termed a 'degradation.'"
(Fehn 2000) Just as his beliefs about the biological inferiority of
people of African descendent undoubtedly shaped American attitudes about race, his beliefs about interracial unions were also likely
significant in shaping attitudes about interracial unions and also
the legal enforcement of this prohibition; laws that as we describe
in Chapter Two were not rendered unconstitutional until 1967.

Perhaps the most devastating aspect of Jefferson's re-conceptualization is not the fact that it is incongruent with this love for a
slave woman nor the fact that he had to jump through ideological
hoops to justify his own behavior, but rather that in making his
justification public, by entering into the realm of public discourse,
a man of such significant influence, indeed a man who would just
a few years later represent the republic as its national leader, most
certainly provided a justification for so many others who might
otherwise have been more liberal on the issue of slavery and on beliefs about the "humanness" of people of African descent. As Therborn argues, the state has the power to establish hegemonic ideology
and to create and modify ideological positions so that they are consistent with the self-interests of the state. Thomas Jefferson, as the
main author on human rights in the new era of the enlightenment,
as author of the Declaration of Independence, as the third President
of the United States, certainly had the power Therborn is talking

about to establish the dominant, hegemonic ideology surrounding the humanness of people of African descent and of slavery as an institution.

David Brion Davis, historian and scholar of slavery, notes the power of this ideology in upholding slavery not only as an economic institution, but also a *moral institution*. Orlando Patterson (1999) details the role that Southern ministers played in the practice of lynching in the period immediately following reconstruction through the 1930s. According to Davis (2006), White Christian Southerners held two contradictory beliefs about race: first, that all humans are descendants of Adam and Eve and second, that people of African descent were inferior and suitable for enslavement. Davis argues that in order to hold such dissonant beliefs during slavery as well as Jim Crow segregation, White Southern Christians revived the Biblical telling of the curse of Ham. (Davis 2006: 187)

Author of the Declaration of Independence and the Statute of Virginia for Religious Freedom, third president of the United States, and founder of the University of Virginia — Jefferson voiced the aspirations of a new America as no other individual of his era. As public official, historian, philosopher, and plantation owner, he served his country for over five decades. And, from this position, it is fair to assume that the White Christian Southerners of whom Davis and Patterson write were influenced by the writings of Jefferson. Though they may not have drawn directly from Jefferson's words, largely because they already held these beliefs, they must have felt vindicated by the perspective of such a powerful man who was known for his forward thinking and "reasoned" approach to questions of morality.

Romantic Relationships: Martha Jefferson

Martha was born October 30, 1748, the daughter of John Wayles and Martha Eppes, wealthy plantation owners in Charles City County, Virginia. Both of her parents had been previously widowed when they met and married. Her mother brought into the marriage, as part of her dowry, a slave named Susanna and her eleven-year-old daughter, Elizabeth Hemings (Betty). After Martha's mother died in 1748, her father remarried. After the death of his third wife, it was widely reported that John Wayles took his slave, Betty, many many years his junior, as his "wife" and that by her he fathered another slave, Sally Hemings. (Thomas Jefferson Foundation: Thomas Jefferson Monticello)

Martha was briefly married to Bathurst Skelton, with whom she had one child. Skelton died in an accident and their son died abruptly of a fever shortly before she met Jefferson.

Thomas Jefferson married Martha Wayles Skelton on January 1, 1772. During their marriage of only ten years, Martha Jefferson bore Thomas Jefferson six children, two surviving into adulthood.

Martha Jefferson died in September 1782, only a few months after the birth of their last child. According to the accounts of the Thomas Jefferson Foundation, she most likely died of childbirth-related health issues. (The White House Biographies) Jefferson was away at the time, but wrote this about learning of Martha's death:

> In his letter, Jefferson refers to " ... the state of dread-
> ful suspense in which I had been kept all the summer and
> the catastrophe which closed it." He goes on to say, "A
> single event wiped away all my plans and left me a blank
> which I had not the spirits to fill up." (Thomas Jeffer-
> son Encyclopedia)

Interracial Relationships

It is widely understood as fact that Thomas Jefferson had a thirty-eight-year relationship with one of his slaves, Sally Hemings, and that she bore him seven children. Though this relationship and the connections between the Jeffersons and the Hemings have been actively denied by the Jeffersons for most of the last 200 years, the relationship was well-known and even documented during Jefferson's life:

Sally Hemings' name became linked to Jefferson's in 1802, when a Richmond newspaper published the allegation that she was Jefferson's mistress and had borne him a number of children. Jefferson's Randolph grandchildren denied the existence of such a relationship, while Sally Hemings' descendants considered their connection to Jefferson an important family truth. Jefferson himself made neither a public response nor any explicit reference to this issue. (Thomas Jefferson Foundation)

Despite Jefferson's silence on the matter, it was a matter of public record that Sally Hemings traveled with Jefferson to France—in fact, some accounts suggest that Jefferson and Hemings were traveling as "husband and wife." (Taylor 2007) Though it is impossible to speculate now, nearly 200 years later, it was not uncommon for African Americans to travel in Europe during slavery and Jim Crow because it offered them a type of freedom of movement that they were denied in the United States.[2] Fehn cites evidence of both the relationship between Jefferson and Hemings and the lure of France that appears in the memoir of Madison Hemings, Sally's daughter:

About the time of [Thomas Jefferson's appointment as minister to France] and before he was ready to leave the country his wife died, and soon after her interment ... he left for France, taking his eldest daughter with him ... [Martha]. The latter [Maria] was left home, but afterwards was ordered to follow him to France. She was three years or so younger than Martha. My mother [Sally Hemings] accompanied her as a body servant ... Their stay (my mother's and Maria's) was about eighteen months. But during that time my mother became Mr. Jefferson's concubine, and when she was called back home she was *enceinte* [i.e. pregnant] by him. He de-

---

2. For example, James Baldwin, Frederick Douglass, Alonzo Herndon, Charles Mingus, Dizzie Gillespie and others experienced far more freedom in Europe—both personally and professionally—than they did in the United States.

sired to bring my mother back to Virginia with him but she demurred. She was just beginning to understand the French language well, and in France she was free, while if she returned to Virginia she would be re-enslaved. So she refused to return with him. To induce her to do so he promised extraordinary privileges, and made a solemn pledge that her children should be freed at the age of twenty-one years. In consequence of his promise … she returned with him to Virginia. Soon after their arrival, she gave birth to a child, of whom Thomas Jefferson was the father. It lived but a short time. She gave birth to four others, and Jefferson was the father of all of them. Their names were Beverly, Harriet, Madison (myself), and Eston—three sons and one daughter. We all became free agreeably to the treaty entered into by our parents before we were born. We all married and have raised families. (Fehn 2000)

With the success of the human genome project, it has been popular for people to explore more fully their ancestry. According to historians like Williamson (1980[1995]) and sociologists like Omi and Winant (1986), a significant percentage of individuals of African descent have mixed ancestry, as a result of both consensual relationships—like that between Jefferson and Hemings—and nonconsensual relationships. Thus, it has been very common for African Americans to use DNA analysis to further examine their racial ancestry. We note here that though obviously these relationships would result in many "Whites" having mixed ancestry, there has been very little interest among Whites' to use DNA analysis to search for their true racial identities. In addition to providing evidence of racial ancestry, these advances in DNA analysis have provided a unique opportunity to establish definitely and scientifically paternity and familial ancestry. The "Black" Jeffersons, as they are often called, took advantage of this opportunity and DNA analysis confirmed that the descendents of Sally Hemings are also the descendents of the Jefferson family. Based on the intimate relationships between Jefferson and Hemings that were widely documented and the lack of a relationship between Hemings and Jefferson's male relatives, the probability that Jefferson fathered Sally Hemings' children is extraordinarily high. (Fehn 2000, Taylor 2007)

After Jefferson's death, several of his slaves, including Hemings and her sons, were able to attain free status. Though many sources report that Jefferson freed Sally Hemings and her sons, according to Gordon-Reed's (2008) laborious and extremely thorough research, only five of Jefferson's slaves were freed by his will. Others were freed by Jefferson's daughter, Martha Randolph, based on his verbal instructions. Others, including several of the Hemings and their relatives, were sold to relatives who were already "free Blacks". Finally, Sally Hemings and her sons were informally emancipated and allowed to move into an apartment in downtown Charlottesville. (Gordon-Reed 2008: 659)

Many of the members of the Hemings family passed into the White community, including Sally Hemings, who was listed as "White" in the 1830 census. Interestingly, according to Gordon-Reed (2008: 659–660), "Her honorary whiteness did not last, however. Three years later, in a special census of 1833, conducted to count the free Blacks in the community for the purposes of determining which of them wanted to be resettled in Africa, Hemings described herself as a "free mulatto."

According to the Thomas Jefferson Foundation, after their mother died, Hemings's sons moved to Ohio and Wisconsin and not only changed their names, replacing "Hemings" with "Jefferson," but also their racial identities. (Thomas Jefferson Foundation) As Staples (2008) noted, Hemings' children actually had more "White than Black ancestry" and had been counted as "White" during the previous census. Not all of the Hemings family passed into the White community and Gordon-Reed identifies this as a major tragedy in Jefferson's legacy. As a result of different emancipation processes— legal emancipation, informal emancipation, the sale of individuals to their family members who were already free—and the refusal of some masters to sell individuals to their family members coupled with different decisions to pass or not pass into the White community, the family was essentially destroyed. (Gordon-Reed 2008)

What makes the Jefferson-Hemings' case that much more interesting—though probably not uncommon—is the fact that, as
noted above, Sally Hemings was Martha Jefferson's (formerly Martha
Wayles) half sister: they shared the same father, John Wayles. There
were several accounts both recorded in the archives of the Thomas
Jefferson Foundation as well as in public records that reported:
"The slave Isaac Jefferson remembered that she [Sally Hemings]
was "mighty near white ... very handsome, long straight hair down
her back" (Thomas Jefferson Foundation) and she bore a striking
resemblance to Jefferson's widow, Martha. Of course, this would not
be surprising given the fact that the women were half-sisters. Thus,
Thomas Jefferson, our Third President and Founding Father, had
two families with half sisters Martha Wayles Jefferson and Sally
Hemings, one the legitimate daughter of John Wayles, the other a
"Black" daughter of John Wayles and his slave.

Conclusion

Jefferson's death merely set the stage for the final cata-
strophe. While history has marveled at the near-simul-
taneous deaths of the Sage of Monticello and the Sage
of Quincy, many years later Peter Fossett, who was still
a young boy when Jefferson died.... understood the
importance of what had happened on July 4, 1826, but
noted that "sorrow came not only to the homes of two
great men ... but to the slaves of Thomas Jefferson." He
was not just talking about the loss of Jefferson. Both
patriots had lived more than their biblical three score and
ten, and human beings are born to die. They are not
born to endure what Fossett and his family endured six
months after the fiftieth anniversary of the signing of
the Declaration of Independence. In January of 1827,
Peter Fossett, all of eleven years old, stood alone on an
auction block and was sold away from his mother, father, brothers and sisters. Fossett's siblings and cousins,

some as young a eight years old, suffered the same fate. (Gordon-Reed 2008: 655)

Jefferson is no doubt one of the most well known, most influential, most studied individuals in American history and indeed around the world. Many would consider Jefferson the "father" of democracy as well as the "father" of human rights. Yet, as others have noted and we have examined here, as forward thinking as Jefferson was, he could not move past the deeply entrenched social, economic and political system that dominated the United States' landscape from its earliest founding some 200 years before his death: slavery. As enlightened as Jefferson was about human rights, he clearly conceptualized these as individual rights—rather than "class rights"—that could be granted—or denied—not only to individual people (for example a person convicted of a crime) but to entire classes of people, including those of African descent. Despite his individual ability to move beyond his ideological beliefs about people of African descent, which is evidenced by the fact that he not only had sexual relations with Sally Hemings, but also seemed to have been in love with her, he could not incorporate these experiences in a way that would allow him to transcend the beliefs and social systems of his time.

This, of course, is true for many people, including several of those we profile in this book. What makes Jefferson unique is not so much the apparent contradictions in his life, but rather the fact that the ideology that he manufactured to ease his own conscience—for example, justifying to himself the fact that he legally owned his romantic partner and their children—was developed and put out for public consumption through Jefferson's access to publishing and thus allowing him to enter these beliefs into public discourse for dissemination and wide consumption.

We close this chapter by challenging readers to re-think their assessment of Jefferson. Though he may very well have been the primary visionary of human rights—the right to life, liberty and the pursuit of happiness—and the architect of the democratic principles we live by today, his inability to envision a United States of America that did not include slavery and the ideology he developed to support this vision is perhaps his most powerful legacy.

Because of his position of power and his privilege as a thinker and writer, Jefferson's personal beliefs about the inferiority of people of African descent were transformed, through his writings, to ideologies and discourses on race that rose to a position of hegemony and significantly shaped the country's laws and attitudes for the nearly 200 years after his death.[3]

Sadly, whereas Jefferson had the opportunity and many personal reasons that would have propelled him toward ending slavery, his fear of a civil war fought over the institution of slavery led not only to another nearly 50 years of slavery, but also to the development of an ideology of race that so widely influenced beliefs and practices that it long out-lasted the institution of slavery itself. Indeed, as many have noted since the historic election of Barack Obama in November of 2008, these same beliefs about the inferiority of individuals of African descent are still held in America strongly enough that the election of a man of African descent led to public displays and expression of racist beliefs.

Jefferson's position in the hierarchy of the leadership of the United States cannot be overlooked. He was not only influential in his thinking and writing but also in how his beliefs were transmitted and accepted by Americans both in his time and now.

Our assessment of his place in American history is not a challenge to his legacy—quite the contrary. Our assessment and contribution to the discussion of Jefferson is an advancement on his legacy that includes what was once an unspoken fact about the man Thomas Jefferson, Third President of the United States.

We believe that Jefferson was irresponsible as a "statesman" when he mouthed and recorded the sentiment that people of African descent were inferior humans, at the same time that he was intimate with Sally Hemings even fathering several children with her. Even

---

3. Jefferson's influence transcended his time: while it is unclear whether he directly influenced Marcus Garvey, the veritable 20th Century Negro leader, it is clear that Garvey latched onto the Jefferson scheme for removing Black slaves from America by sending them back to Africa. (Grant 2008)

at the time of his death, when he could have formally emancipated his romantic partner and his children, he chose not to, because, according to Gordon-Reed (2008: 659):

> Jefferson's will had both public and private dimensions. It was a public document, with a public effect, but it was also a last statement to Martha Randolph [his daughter] and his legal white grandchildren. It is all but impossible that any but the youngest among them in 1826 would *not* have known about Jefferson and Hemings. As in all families, knowing and keeping secrets within the family is one thing. There is little doubt that Jefferson and the Randolphs would have seen a public indication that he did indeed have a "shadow family" as deep betrayal of his legal one … The way Sally Hemings departed Monticello is, then, a study in avoidance. It avoided harm to Jefferson's legacy, it avoided further embarrassment to his white family …

He was, like others we chronicle in this book, a hypocrite.

Jefferson died at Monticello on July 4, 1826, the 50th anniversary of the signing of the Declaration of Independence and less than forty years before the Civil War and the signing of the Emancipation Proclamation in 1862 by President Abraham Lincoln.

Chapter Four

George Washington: Founding Father of the United States, Father of a Slave?

George Washington, one of the founding fathers of the United States and its first president, was an affluent White man who was typical of his time. A Southern planter from Virginia, Washington ran his plantation, Mount Vernon, with the labor of slaves. In addition, there is speculation that he also fathered his only child with a slave. This speculation is based primarily on oral history and has not been confirmed by a DNA analysis.

Early Life

George Washington was born in 1732 to a Virginia planter family. At age 16, he helped to survey the Shenandoah Valley and by age 22 (1754), he was commissioned as a lieutenant colonel. His first opportunities to fight involved the early skirmishes that would later become the French and Indian Wars.

Professional Life

From 1759 until the outbreak of the American Revolutionary War, Washington, who had married the widow Martha Dandridge Custis, managed his land around Mount Vernon. Like many others, Washington felt exploited by the British colonial system and attended the Second Continental Congress in Philadelphia in 1775 as a delegate from Virginia. He was appointed commander and chief of the continental army while at the Continental Congress. He forced the surrender of British General Cornwallis in 1781 and with the war over he longed to return to Mount Vernon. However, the young nation was not functioning well, and Washington attended the Constitutional Convention in Philadelphia in 1787 where he was unanimously elected as the nation's first president. He served as president from 1789–1797 after which he retired to Mount Vernon where he died, less than three years later, December 14, 1799. (http://www.whitehouse.gov/history/presidents/gw1.html)

The Paternity Case against George Washington

According to Linda Allen Bryant, in her recent book *I Cannot Tell a Lie: The True Story of George Washington's African American Descendants* (2004), Washington had a sexual liaison with his brother's mulatto woman slave, Venus, around 1748. Venus' child, West Ford, is believed to be the son of George Washington. Bryant, a direct descendent of West Ford, bases her assertion that Ford was fathered by a sexual liaison between his mother, Venus, and the father of the United States, George Washington, on more than two hundred years of oral tradition in the Ford Family. Specifically, she builds her case by using records of Washington's visit to his brother John's plantation, as well as evidence that Ford was afforded special treatment by Washington himself before he died and by the Mount Vernon estate after Washington's death.

According to Pompeian (March 31 2005), who reviewed Bryant's book for George Mason University's *History News Network*, the paternity claim leveled against Washington first emerged in print as early as the 1940s, though it gained support following the DNA tests that confirmed Thomas Jefferson's paternity of at least one child born by Sally Hemings (see Chapter Three).

According to Bryant (2004), Ford's mother, the mulatto slave Venus, was a house slave and personal attendant to Washington's sister-in-law, Hannah Washington. According to the Ford family oral tradition, after Ford was born, Venus confided in her mistress that George Washington was Ford's father. The Ford family oral traditions are filled with stories—and Washington's diary confirms this—that in the decade prior to his presidency, Washington was a frequent visitor to his brother's plantation, Bushfield Plantation, and during his visits Ford was assigned as his personal attendant; Ford even attended church with Washington and they were seated in a private pew. (Ford n.d.) All of the records indicate that Washington's contact with Ford ceased upon his ascension to the presidency. (Ford n.d.)

After John Washington's death, West Ford remained the property of Washington's family and continued working on the Bushfield Plantation. He became the property of Hannah Washington, his mother's mistress, who decreed in her last will and testament of 1802 that Ford was to be freed on his 21st birthday, which he was, around 1806. (Ford n.d.) According to both the Ford family records and the records of Mount Vernon, the occasion of Ford's emancipation is cause for an official portrait of Ford painted by the Mount Vernon portraitist. (Vernon n.d.)

Because George Washington had no legitimate children, after Martha Washington's death, George Washington's nephew, Bushrod Washington, John Washington's son, inherited Mount Vernon. (He also inherited the Bushfield plantation after the death of his father, John Washington.) Upon his death, Bushrod Washington (George Washington's nephew), willed 160 acres of land adjacent to Mount Vernon to Ford. (Ford n.d.; Vernon n.d.) Ford and his family (he married and had four children) lived and worked at Mount Vernon and his children were educated there, despite laws that specifically prohibited the education of slaves and their descendents. (Ford n.d.) Ford and his family are credited with founding one of the first settlements of freed Blacks in Virginia: Gum Springs, Virginia. (Ford n.d.; Vernon n.d.)

George Washington's Views on Race and Slavery

George Washington was born into the highly stratified slave-plantation economy of the early 18th century Southern U.S. colony of Virginia. According to official biographers of Washington at Mount Vernon, in the early part of his life, Washington accepted slavery unequivocally. (Vernon n.d.) Washington became a slave owner at age eleven (1743) when his father died and he inherited all of his father's "property," including a 500-acre plantation and ten slaves. (Vernon n.d.)

Washington continued to acquire slaves through their own reproduction, through his marriage to Martha Custis—who brought twenty slaves with her when she moved to Mount Vernon—and by the time of his death in 1799, Washington owned 316 slaves on the Mount Vernon estate. (Vernon n.d.)

Biographers of Washington and curators of his papers at Mount Vernon seem to agree that Washington's views of slavery changed as he aged, and that he "became increasingly conscious of the contradiction between the struggle to establish the first nation-state based on the principles of democracy and the system of slavery." (Vernon n.d.) However, for a variety of reasons, both individual and collective, Washington never engaged in a public fight against slavery. Curators of his estate at Mount Vernon conclude that his reluctance to speak out publicly against slavery derived from his belief that to do so would isolate Southerners and ultimately tear apart a nation he had worked so hard to build. (Vernon n.d.) These experts argue further that Washington's decision to include a dictate in his will to free his slaves upon the death of his wife indicated his awareness of the dissonance between his attitudes (antislavery) and his behaviors (owning slaves). (Vernon n.d.)

As Twohig (2001) notes, there is much debate about whether Washington's views on slavery were based on his increasing moral abhorrence of the practice or his evaluation that it was not economically sufficient. (Vernon n.d.)

It is evident that Washington expressed his private opinions rather widely. Francis Asbury, first bishop of the Methodist Church in America, for example, visited Mount Vernon in 1785 and noted in his diary that General Washington had given his visitors "his opinion against slavery." But whatever his changing views, Washington, like many of his antislavery contemporaries, still let his own economic interests rule when they interfered with his principles. Not only did he still need slaves to work his own plantation, he must have been at least somewhat aware that much of the golden age of economic and social expansion in the Chesapeake had rested on Black bondsmen. Washington himself was an avid partaker in the Anglicization of Chesapeake society with its emphasis on creature comforts and the acquisition of consumer goods, much of which was dependent on a slave economy. In fact it is difficult to discern from his meager comments whether Washington's disgust with slavery rests on moral grounds (although there are some indications that this is so) or primarily on the grounds of the institution's economic inefficiencies. Although he probably never exposed his sentiments to the wrenching self-examination that Jefferson did, it is reasonable to project to Washington at least some of Jefferson's painful attempts to justify the inconsistencies of preaching freedom for the rebelling colonies and still defend the fetters that kept another race enslaved. Jefferson's moral struggles, even if, as Bernard Bailyn suggests, they led him into a reluctant and apologetic racism, are more enlightening than Washington's, if only because we know more about them. (Twohig 2001)

Others, ourselves included, view Washington's decision to free his slaves after the death of his wife as less virtuous and more directly self-interested. (Twohig 2001) One can argue, for example, that Washington's decision to free his slaves after his wife's death was "easy" in that it allowed him to preserve a privileged standard of living for himself and his family (he and Martha had no children) while simultaneously allowing him to contribute to the perception of others that he was committed to equality and freedom in his new America.

> Washington shared the determination of most of his own generation of statesmen not to allow slavery to disturb their agenda for the new Republic. Antislavery sentiment came in a poor second when it conflicted with the powerful economic interests of proslavery forces. To Washington as to many Americans, even some whose opinions on slavery were far more radical than his own, the institution had become a subject so divisive that public comments were best left unsaid. Washington himself was far from being an egalitarian. In spite of the Revolution's rhetoric, the United States was still a society of deference and Washington never seriously questioned the political and social validity of the prevailing ideas of rule by an elite any more than he questioned his own position in such a society. Publicly no comments came from him on slavery. For Washington, as for most of the other founders, when the fate of the new republic was balanced against his own essentially conservative opposition to slavery, there was really no contest. (Twohig 2001)

Conclusion

Historians may never be able to separate the fact from the fiction in the West Ford story or in Linda Allen Bryant's book. Regardless, *I Cannot Tell a Lie* is an important reminder of the sexual, ethical, and racial double standards found in American slavery. Whether true or false, Bryant's book is another addition to the canon of slave history that highlights the dark realities of the plantation culture. (*Pompeian* March 31 2005)

Though the details of interracial liaisons are important, Pompeian's quote sums it up rather well. It is of less importance whether West Ford's father is George Washington—as the Ford family claims—or John Washington, George's brother—as the historians at Mount Vernon claim—than the fact that many of the very men who founded the United States on the renegade principles of equality were able to simultaneously hold these perspectives while owning the women they had sexual relations with and the children they fathered. Of course in the context of the 17th and 18th centuries, White men owned all human beings, including White women. However, the contrast provided by slavery and the intimacy of sexual relationships and paternity with slave women who were considered not only irrational and incapable—as White women were—but less than fully human exposes both the power of the ideology of racial domination, as well as some of the underlying reasons for the segregation apparatus of miscegenation: the requirement Whites developed specifically to mark and reinforce the racial boundary, and by restricting the only "legitimate" crossings to themselves, thus reminding African Americans of their second class citizenship. (Epstein 2007; Hattery 2008; Smith and Hattery 2009)

Chapter Five

Richard Mentor Johnson: The Interracial "Marriage" of the Vice-President

Introduction

Richard Mentor Johnson is not a particularly well-known figure from United States history—in fact, the majority of Americans have probably never even heard of him. We first learned of Richard Mentor Johnson from a colleague who is a historian of the U.S. South and who suggested we explore Johnson's life. We include a chapter on Johnson not only because he had an interracial marriage while achieving one of the highest offices in the land (the vice-presidency), but also because his biography offers a different story than those of his "predecessors," George Washington and Thomas Jefferson.

Early Life

Richard Johnson was born in 1780 in an area near modern-day Louisville which was, at the time of his birth, an outpost of Virginia. His family was prosperous and by the time he was entering adulthood, his father, Robert Johnson, was one of the largest landholders in the state of Kentucky. (Senate n.d.)

Professional Life

Richard Mentor Johnson served as the United States' ninth vice-president during the administration of President Martin Van Buren, 1837–1841. Johnson was elected vice-president by the senate, the only time this process has ever been invoked, as a result of the fact that no vice-presidential candidate received a clear majority. When this situation arises, the 12th amendment to the U.S. Constitution allows the U.S. Senate to select between the two individuals receiving the most votes. In addition to serving as vice-president, Johnson's career in Congress — both the House and the Senate — spanned three decades. He was a controversial member of congress for many reasons but is perhaps most well-known for " … the dubious claim that he killed the Shawnee chieftain Tecumseh in 1813 at the Battle of the Thames." (Senate n.d.)

Johnson's Interracial Marriage

According to several sources, including the official Senate guide to public officials, for at least three decades, Johnson had an open, committed, and co-habiting intimate relationship with a mulatto slave, Julia Chinn. (2003) Their first child was born in 1804, so we can presume their relationship began sometime before that and lasted until Julia died of cholera in 1833. (2003; Senate n.d.) Julia was "raised" by Johnson's mother and Johnson inherited her when his father died. (Senate n.d.)

Johnson and Julia had two daughters, "Adeline, born October 13, 1804, and Imogene, born February 17, 1812. Legally, they were African Americans and Johnson's slave property." (2003) Yet, by all accounts Johnson's relationship with Julia and his daughters was authentic, sincere and no different from any other family (2003; Senate n.d.), except, of course, for the fact that Johnson and Julia could never legally marry due to the anti-miscegenation laws that barred the legal marriage between any White and non-White person.

Though people in Johnson's community apparently accepted his relationship with Julia, the racial identities of their children clearly were the site of contested terrain. One source recounts the following incident, which is illustrative of the complexities of racial identity in the slave South:

> Invited one year to deliver a Fourth of July oration, Johnson sent his daughters to the pavilion where the White ladies were seated. The ladies forced them to move. An angry Johnson rushed through his speech, picked up his daughters, and quickly departed. (2003)

Despite the sometimes contentiousness surrounding the racial identity of Johnson's daughters, both married White men and upon Johnson's death, inherited equal tracts of Johnson's estate. (2003) After Julia's death in 1833, it is reported that Johnson had several "mulatto mistresses." (Senate n.d.)

Johnson's Politics

Though Johnson's family was rich and powerful, and indeed through the inheritance of land and slaves Johnson became rich himself, he never identified with the aristocracy. And, though we have little of his writing or speeches to analyze for his perspective on matters of stratification and equality (or inequality), Johnson's actions provide some insight. For example, his biographers have noted that he often waived fees for indigent clients. (Senate n.d.) It is also well documented that Johnson set up an "Indian" school on his property and the teacher he hired, James Y. Henderson, was also a strong proponent of educating Blacks. He spent time each week in Johnson's home teaching not only his daughters but also the house slaves to read the Bible. (2003)

Unlike some of the other political figures discussed in this book— ie. Clarence Thomas Jefferson or Strom Thurmond—Johnson's life is not filled with extraordinary contradictions, rather it is illustrative of the contradictions inherent in the Southern slave plantation economy of the 17th, 18th, and 19th centuries. For example,

Johnson's household included his own mixed-race children, who under the "one drop rule" (Johnston 1970) would have been categorized as "Black," as well as house slaves of the same age (and perhaps complexion). One set of children he "owned" and the other he did not. This situation in and of itself is rife with contradictions but is also reflective of the typical plantation household.

Johnson's life is also illustrative of the type of community, Central Point, Caroline County, Virginia, where the Lovings grew up. As noted in Chapter Two, Central Point, Virginia was a visibly mixed-race community and interracial relationships and mixed-race people were widely accepted. (Staples 2008) Similarly, by all accounts, Johnson's personal life and his common-law interracial marriage and mixed-race children only became problematic when he became a U.S. Senator with a statewide constituency and thus he was subjected to a wider public gaze. This is in contrast to the little attention his personal life received when he was a member of the House, representing a smaller, tightly knit congressional district. (Senate n.d.)

Conclusion

What sets Johnson apart from other men of his day are two rather simple but complex facts: his vice-presidency and his "marriage" to his slave. As many historians have noted, it was extremely common for White, Southern planters to have sexual liaisons with the female slaves on their plantations. In fact, these liaisons are most likely the primary source of the "mulatto" race, which Williamson documents as comprising more than one-tenth of the African American population and 2 percent of the total U.S. population according to the 1850 census. (Williamson [1980] 1995) What is unique about Johnson's relationship with Julia Chinn is that he acknowledged it openly, lived in the relationship just as if the couple were legally married, and raised his children, who were a product of this interracial relationship. And, though there were many communities like Central Point, Caroline County, Virginia, that openly accepted interracial families and mixed-race people, there were very few national figures who openly acknowledged these relationships. As we see in the cases of both Thomas Jefferson and Strom Thurmond, though people in their families and communities clearly knew about their interracial relationships with women of African descent, they married White women, raised "White" families, and they kept their interracial relationships outside of Washington.

Though Johnson may not have been actively part of the anti-slavery movement of the early 19th century, his personal life provides illustrations of his commitment to fairness; specifically his treatment of his daughters both in terms of their racial identity but also in his decision to pass down his property to them upon his death. This is unusual not only because of race, but also because of gender. Perhaps Johnson's commitment to fairness, expressed primarily in his support for government policies that were designed to bring relief to the poor (Senate n.d.), would also have extended to matters of race had he lived in the post-Civil War era. We will never know.

AN AFFECTING SCENE IN KENTUCKY.

Complete Explanation

A racist attack on Democratic vice-presidential candidate Richard M. Johnson. The Kentucky Congressman's nomination, in May 1835, as

Van Buren's running-mate for the 1836 election raised eyebrows even among party faithful, because of Johnson's common-law marriage to a mulatto woman, Julia Chinn, by whom he fathered two daughters. The artist ridicules Johnson's domestic situation, and the Democrats' constituency as well.

Seated in a chair with his hand over his face, a visibly distraught Johnson lets a copy of James Watson Webb's "New York Courier and Enquirer" fall to the floor and moans, "When I read the scurrilous attacks in the Newspapers on the Mother of my Children, pardon me, my friends if I give way to feelings!!! My dear Girls, bring me your Mother's picture, that I may show it to my friends here." On the right are his two daughters, Adeline and Imogene, wearing elegant evening dresses. One presents a painting of a black woman wearing a turban, and says, "Here it is Pa, but don't take on so." The second daughter says, "Poor dear Pa, how much he is affected." A man behind them exclaims, "Pickle! Pop!! and Ginger!!! Can the slayer of Tecumseh be thus overcome like a summer cloud! Fire and Furies. Oh!" Johnson is reported to have slain the Indian chief Tecumseh.

Flanking Johnson are a gaunt abolitionist (right) and a black man. The abolitionist holds a copy of the "Emancipator," a Hartford, Connecticut newspaper, and says, "Be comforted Richard; all of us abolitionists will support thee." The black man pledges, " ... de honor of a Gentlemen dat all de Gentlemen of Colour will support you."

On the far left is a stout postmaster who says, "Your Excellency, I am sure all of us Postmasters and deputies will stick to you; if you promise to keep us in office."

The print seems to date from early in the campaign of 1836. Johnson's wife Julia Chinn died in 1833. Adeline, one of the two daughters pictured, died in February 1836. Although Weitenkampf dates the print at 1840, when Johnson was again Van Buren's running-mate, the presence of both daughters and the drawing style are persuasive evidence for an 1836 date.

Source: Harpers Weekly, American Political Prints, 1766–1876

http://loc.harpweek.com/LCPoliticalCartoons/IndexDisplayCartoonMedium.asp?SourceIndex=People&IndexText=Chinn%2C+Julia&UniqueID=5&Year=1836

Chapter Six

Frederick Douglass: Abolitionist and Feminist, "Walking the Walk"

Frederick Douglass is one of the best-known African Americans in U.S. history. Born into slavery, Douglass became free in 1838, when he entered the free state of New York. He attended his first anti-slavery convention in 1841 and from that time forward dedicated his life to working for freedom and social justice, not just for the end of slavery, but also for equality for women.

Douglass's Early Life

Douglass was born into slavery in the early 1800s. In his auto-biography he writes:

> Frederick Douglass was born in slavery as Frederick Au-gustus Washington Bailey near Easton in Talbot County, Maryland. He was not sure of the exact year of his birth, but he knew that it was 1817 or 1818. (Douglass 1845)

He barely knew his mother, and notes that it was commonplace on Maryland plantations for slave mothers to be separated from their children before the age of 12 months, though because he was raised by his grandmother, he knew something about his parents. His mother was the daughter of two slaves and she was very dark com-plected, darker than either of her parents. (Douglass 1845) With re-gard to his father, Douglass writes:

> My father was a white man. He was admitted to be such by all I ever heard speak of my parentage. The opin-ion was also whispered that my master was my father;

but of the correctness of this opinion, I know nothing; the means of knowing was withheld from me. (Douglass 1845)

At the age of eight, Douglass was sent to Baltimore to live with his former master's son-in-law, Mr. Hugh Auld. His mistress, Sophia Auld, taught him his "ABC" (Douglass 1845) though his "training" was interrupted when his master found out and forbid her from teaching Douglass because he believed that with an education, Douglass would no longer be fit for slavery. In his reflections on life as a slave in Baltimore, Douglass remarks that city slaves had considerably more freedom than plantation slaves and this created many opportunities, among them the chance to continue his education by befriending White boys he met on the street and enlisting their help. (Douglass 1845)

After several years of working for various masters in Baltimore and St. Michaels, Douglass was hired out as a caulker. Still a slave, he had to pay his master his wage. Two or three years into this arrangement, Douglass, who had been obsessed by freedom since the age of twelve, escaped and fled to the free state of New York. Thus, by age 20, in 1838, Douglass was free. (Douglass 1845) He immediately sent word to a woman he had known on the plantation in Maryland, the free-woman Anna Murray, and on September 15, 1838, they were married.

Douglass's Political Writings

Douglass is perhaps the most well known African American abolitionist. Though its clear from his autobiography (Douglass 1845) that Douglass began asking questions and making observations about slavery as a young child, his decision to devote his life to the dismantling of slavery probably began in 1841, when Douglass attended an antislavery conference in Nantucket, Massachusetts, and this ignited in him the desire to write and lecture about the horrors of slavery. He became a key figure in the abolitionist movement where he met many other intellectuals and social organizers, including Elizabeth Cady Stanton, with whom he would forge a long friendship and begin his work for women's equality.[1]

Perhaps Douglass' most well-known and oft-cited speech about the politics of slavery and race in America is entitled "The Meaning of the Fourth of July for the Negro." (Douglass n.d.) As if addressing Thomas Jefferson himself, Douglass lays out the inherent contradictions in the Declaration of Independence and indeed the very establishment of the United States of America on the principles of equality while simultaneously engaging in the inhumane system of chattel slavery.

> I say it with a sad sense of the disparity between us. I am not included within the pale of glorious anniversary! Your high independence only reveals the immeasurable distance between us. The blessings in which you, this day, rejoice, are not enjoyed in common. The rich inheritance of justice, liberty, prosperity and independence, bequeathed by your fathers, is shared by you, not by me. The sunlight that brought light and healing to you, has brought stripes and death to me. This Fourth July is yours, not mine. You may rejoice, I must mourn. To drag a man in fetters into the grand illuminated temple of liberty, and call upon him to join you in joyous anthems, were inhuman mockery and sacrilegious irony. Do you mean, citizens, to mock me, by asking me to speak to-day? If so, there is a parallel to your conduct. And let me warn you that it is dangerous to copy the example of a nation whose crimes, towering up to

---

1. Douglass and Stanton worked for many years out of their headquarters in Rochester, New York. Their relationship was irreparably damaged over the fight for the Fourteenth Amendment. White elites made it clear that only one group (African Americans or women) would walk through the door and be granted the right to vote. For a variety of reasons, Republican politicians were more amenable to granting African American men the right to vote than women of any race or ethnicity. Stanton urged Douglass to seek the right to vote for all or none, and his unwillingness to leave the abolitionist movement for the suffrage movement ended their long friendship and working relationship.

heaven, were thrown down by the breath of the Almighty, burying that nation in irrevocable ruin! I can to-day take up the plaintive lament of a peeled and woe-smitten people! ... What, to the American slave, is your 4th of July? I answer; a day that reveals to him, more than all other days in the year, the gross injustice and cruelty to which he is the constant victim. To him, your celebration is a sham; your boasted liberty, an unholy license; your national greatness, swelling vanity; your sounds of rejoicing are empty and heartless; your denunciation of tyrants, brass fronted impudence; your shouts of liberty and equality, hollow mockery; your prayers and hymns, your sermons and thanksgivings, with all your religious parade and solemnity, are, to Him, mere bombast, fraud, deception, impiety, and hypocrisy—a thin veil to cover up crimes which would disgrace a nation of savages. There is not a nation on the earth guilty of practices more shocking and bloody than are the people of the United States, at this very hour. (Douglass n.d.)

Clearly, Douglass is agitating not only for the end of slavery, but also for the dismantling of the system of racial domination on which it is built. Furthermore, he articulates the strangeness that the core ideology from which the United States is born is in such contradiction to the use of chattel slave labor on which the Unites States is actually built. Douglass also noted, as perhaps only an "outsider"—a non-White person—could the negative impact that this inhumane form of chattel slavery had on Whites. Reflecting on his mistress in Baltimore he writes:

Slavery proved as injurious to her as it did to me. When I went there, she was a pious, warm, and tender-hearted woman. There was no sorrow or suffering for which she had not a tear. She had bread for the hungry, clothes for the naked, and comfort for every mourner that came within her reach. Slavery soon proved its ability to divest her of these heavenly qualities. (Douglass 1845)

Douglass may also be one of the first to suggest that only through intimate relationships between the races will true equality be available. In his speech "The Future of the Colored Race" Douglass asserts most clearly his attitudes about interracial relationships (Douglass n.d.):

> My strongest conviction as to the future of the negro therefore is, that he will not be expatriated nor annihilated, nor will he forever remain a separate and distinct race from the people around him, but that he will be absorbed, assimilated, and will only appear finally, as the Phoenicians now appear on the shores of the Shannon, in the features of a *blended race [emphasis is ours]*.

We suggest that its quite possible that Douglass' attitude is in part shaped by the fact that his father, who was a White planter, never seemed to have any contact with his mother, a slave, except for impregnating her, which is as likely to have been consensual as nonconsensual. This experience, coupled with his own interest in interracial relationships (of which he eventually had at least two) clearly shaped his beliefs about race, intimacy, and equality for people of African descent.

Interracial Marriage

Frederick's marriage to Anna Murray Douglass lasted for 44 years, until she died in 1882. Eighteen months later, he married Helen Pitts, his secretary, who just happened to be White and twenty years Douglass' junior.

Pitts and Douglass met when Pitts moved to Uniontown, New York, to live with her uncle, whose home was next door to Douglass'. Pitts was a long-time activist in the women's suffrage movement and it was this interest that drew her and Douglass into conversation. (Douglass n.d.)

Though it seems an unlikely union, and though many on both sides expressed their discontent, in many ways Pitts was exactly the type of woman suited for a relationship with Douglass. Why? Because she was a woman of privilege and because she grew up in a family committed to racial equality. (Douglass n.d.) There is recent and compelling evidence to suggest that Pitts was not the first White woman of privilege with whom Douglass had a relationship. According to scholars at the Gilder Lehrman Center for the Study of Slavery, Resistance, and Abolition, Douglass carried on a 20-year intimate, sexual relationship with another White woman of privilege, German abolitionist Ottilie Assing. (Soskis n.d.) Soskis further asserts that it was the stark contrasts between Anna Douglass, Frederick's wife, and women like Assing and later Pitts that caused internal strife for Douglass. Specifically Soskis notes that many contemporaries of Douglass, particularly his abolitionist colleagues in Europe, noted that Anna was dark, illiterate and inarticulate whereas the White women he had relationships with were not only educated but privileged. Based on some letters between Douglass and his British colleagues, Soskis argues that it was Anna's character and Douglass' recognition that she would never be accepted into British society in the manner in which he was that was the key reason he never moved the family to Europe. Furthermore, because Anna had helped to finance his freedom, he felt indebted to her and thus deferred his marriage to a White woman until after she died. (Soskis n.d.)

Pitts was born in 1838 in Honeoye, New York. Her parents were staunch abolitionists. She was educated at Mount Holyoke and immediately after graduation took a job teaching at Hampton Institute, now Hampton University, which was in the 1800s a "college for Negroes." (Douglass n.d.)

Not only was Pitts an educated woman, which was a mark of her privilege, but she was a cousin to two former presidents of the United States: John Adams and John Quincy Adams. (Douglass n.d.) The types of circles that Pitts moved in — White, liberal, and privileged — were exactly the same types of circles that Douglass was aligned with; a typical pattern for those African Americans of the 19th century who were involved in any aspect of the movement for racial equality. This is, for example, similar to the experience of Booker T. Washington, whose major benefactor was the funder of the Tuskegee Institute, Andrew Carnegie.

Thus, marrying only 20 years after the official end of slavery, in a time that was characterized not only by high levels of segregation but also incredible social distance between Whites and African Americans, these associations between liberal affluent Whites and free African Americans, all of whom were working on issues of racial justice, were common and thus the relationship between Douglass and Pitts is not all that surprising. In her obituary it is written:

> The companionship grew to friendship and sympathy, perhaps more. Certainly Helen Pitts, a highly cultured and mature woman of 45, knew her own mind when she married the ex-slave. Mrs. Douglass had a dignified self-possession which carried her serenely and harmoniously through every difficult situation and sustained her double relationship to races between whom was growing up a social antagonism unknown in earlier days when the intellectual giants of the North took every pains to identify themselves in interest and sympathy with their Black brother. Whether Helen Pitts married Mr. Douglass in the hope to help make a bridge across which cultured souls might cross to each other regardless of the accident of color, or whether it was from purely personal reasons we may not know. The only clue she ever gave me was once when she said, "Regarding Mr. Douglass as I did I should have been a coward not to have married him." (Douglass n.d.)

Thus, the marriage between Douglass and Pitts is interesting on many different levels. The writer of the obituary implies that Pitts' decision to marry Douglass may be have been political, an attempt to "walk the walk" not just "talk the talk." Yet, what about for Douglass? Certainly he was interested in and did build successful alliances with Whites, including such influential people of the time as William Lloyd Garrison and Elizabeth Cady Stanton. However, whereas Pitts might have been praised for reaching across the color line to enter into the most intimate of relationships with an African American man, Douglass' decision to do so would most certainly have been interpreted differently. It is likely that many African Americans at the time might have called Douglass a "race traitor" or accused him of "sleeping with the enemy," because entering an intimate relationship with a White woman was not only dangerous for an African American man, as tens of thousands of African American men were lynched simply on the prospect of this (Davis 1983; Patterson 1999), but also because it might be considered one thing for a Black man to pander to White philanthropists of the time but quite another to enter into an intimate union with a White person.

Furthermore, despite many close relationships between Whites and African Americans in these social networks, there are no other examples of interracial marriages like that between Pitts and Douglass. As scholars of contemporary race relations such as Eduardo Bonilla-Silva (2001, 2003) note, there is typically a long distance between racial attitudes and behavioral practices, especially among Whites. Thus, it is not surprising that the union between Pitts and Douglass drew criticism from both sides. Douglass himself wrote:

> Some blacks, and many whites, criticized him for marrying outside his race, but Douglass categorically rejected the notion that his actions should be constrained by his skin color. For him the marriage symbolized one more victory in his lifelong crusade against racial discrimination. (Douglass n.d.)

This last comment in Douglass' passage reveals that perhaps he, like Helen Pitts, saw their union as an opportunity to break down racial barriers at the most intimate level: by marrying. So, though Douglass may have been considered a race traitor by some, his own assessment is that this act symbolized something much bigger: a victory against racial discrimination and segregation. And, of course, this is consistent with his remarks on interracial marriage quoted above.

Conclusion

The issues surrounding the marriage between Douglass and Pitts are complex and interesting, especially when we compare their union to many of the others we have written about thus far. Like Johnson, Douglass' relationship is public. In contrast, Johnson was unable to marry Julia because of anti-miscegenation laws in Kentucky, whereas Douglass was able to marry Pitts because New York never enacted legal prohibitions against interracial unions. Though our knowledge of these interracial unions is limited to what is written about them and preserved in public records, every account of Johnson's relationship to Julia includes statements about his love for her and his devotion to their family. In contrast, as seen in the historical data included here, the discussion of Douglass' union with Pitts is always couched in political terms and there is never any mention of love. Whether this is accurate or not is impossible to discern. But, it raises interesting questions about the ways in which interracial relationships of public figures are described by those observing at the time—in newspaper accounts, obituaries, and political cartoons. Either way, the mere fact that there is anything written in the public discourse about the interracial relationships any of these men—Washington, Jefferson, Johnson or Douglass—had is indicative of their rarity and the contentious nature of these relationships.

Finally, we note that without exception, each of the African Americans—men or women—involved in these interracial unions were "mulatto." Given Williamson's (Williamson [1980] 1995) estimate that 10 percent of the African American population in the 1860 census was categorized as mulatto, it is striking that in 100 percent of the cases we've examined here involving White men with political clout and public lives who were involved in interracial relationships, their partners were always mulatto. Added to this is the fact that Douglass himself was mulatto. This raises an entirely different set of questions around at least two key issues: the differential treatment of "mulatto" slaves—as house slaves and personal "attendants" as opposed to field slaves, their likelihood of becoming educated, (Blassingame 1979) — as well as Whites' attitudes about mulattos as compared to those of purely African or African American descent. Fast forward to the 21st century and we note that the first "Black" President of the United States of America, Barack Obama, is himself of mixed-race heritage: he is a mulatto. That these important issues are raised in a book ostensibly about interracial intimate couplings elucidates just how contested they are and how deeply embedded these relationships are in the fabric of American life.

Chapter Seven

Clarence Thomas, "Protector" of Civil Rights in the 21st Century

> I don't see my husband as Black.
> Ginni Thomas on interracial marriage

Introduction

Clarence Thomas was born June 23, 1948, into the segregated southern community of Pin Point, Georgia. When he was 10 years old, the landmark desegregation case *Brown v. Board of Education* was decided by the same court Thomas would later join, and ironically from which he would render decisions that effectively turned back many of the important outcomes that arose from the *Brown* decision. Thomas was educated in the top private universities in the country; he earned his bachelor's degree from Holy Cross and his law degree from Yale. Clarence Thomas, appointed to the court by President George H. W. Bush in 1991, is only the second African American to sit on the United States Supreme Court, the highest court in the land. Justice Thomas replaced the late Justice Thurgood Marshall who retired from the Court in 1991 and died January 24, 1993. Ironically, the justice Thomas replaced, Justice Thurgood Marshall, was one of the primary lawyers who argued the *Brown* case, the very same case that Thomas has spent the last two decades dismantling. (Thomas 2007) It is these types of contradictions that make Thomas an interesting case for inquiry.

Thomas' Early Life

Clarence Thomas' early life clearly shaped his professional life, but perhaps not in the ways one would expect. Thomas is the second child born to Leola and M.C. Thomas. Though there is some discrepancy in the record keeping, both were teenagers at the time of his birth—in fact, all three of their children were born before either turned 20. Because of disinterest and neglect on the part of his young mother and a wandering spirit on the part of his father, his parents divorced before Clarence was three. (Merida and Fletcher 2007) Not only was Thomas' immediate family life dismal, life in Pin Point, though filled with adventure and several key extended family members, held little hope. According to Thomas biographers Kevin Merida and Michael Fletcher, Pin Point, Georgia has a population of fewer than 300 people (272), no stores, industries, or jobs, no public schools—local children are bused to a neighboring school district—and 80 percent of the residents live below the poverty line. (Merida and Fletcher 2007) Pin Point, Georgia, is so small that we were unable to find any demographic data specific to Pin Point in the U.S. Census. To paraphrase the words of Hall of Fame baseball player, Kirby Puckett, Pin Point is a place where Hope Dies.[1] It's clear that Thomas' early life was difficult and filled with barriers.

In the fall of 1954, Thomas' life would change in many critical ways. First of all, he started school, beginning the first grade just four months after the landmark *Brown* decision, in the *segregated* Haven Home school.[1] Shortly after beginning the first grade, Thomas' home tragically burned down, an accidental fire started by

---

1. Puckett is actually referring to the public housing projects in Chicago where he grew up: Robert Taylor Homes.

2. Contrary to what many Northerners like one of the authors believe and were taught in school, the battle to integrate or desegregate schools lasted for nearly 20 years, with most districts not integrating until the early 1970s and only under the auspices of forced bussing programs. Douglas, Davidson M. 1995. *Reading, Writing, & Race: The Desegregation of the Charlotte Schools.* Chapel Hill, North Carolina: University of North Carolina Press.

his younger brother and a friend who were trying to light a gas heater. As a result, Thomas and his siblings were separated. He, along with his younger brother, moved with their mother to Savannah where Leola found a job as a maid " ... earning $15 a week and rented a shabby one-room tenement with an outdoor toilet." (Merida and Fletcher 2007: 51)

Savannah

Many of Thomas' childhood friends as well as his biographers note that the story that Thomas likes to tell about himself and that others like to tell about him focuses on his very early life in Pin Point, Georgia. This telling of his history helps us to substantiate the Horatio Alger myth. And, though we can argue about which years are the core of a person's "formative years," Thomas actually spent most of his childhood and young adult life living a middle class lifestyle in Savannah.

Not long after moving into the one-room tenement, by the summer of 1955, Thomas' mother, struggling as a single mother to raise two sons, asked her father for help. Her stepmother, Christine, persuaded Thomas' grandfather that the children should move in with them, and that was the beginning of a new life for Thomas. (Merida and Fletcher 2007)

Moving in with his grandfather opened many doors of opportunity for Thomas. Not only did he find a safe and secure home in which to live and plentiful portions of healthy food on the table, but Thomas' grandfather paid for his private, Catholic school education and introduced him to the local library, a place Thomas would spend countless hours while he was growing up as a way to avoid working with his grandfather or doing chores around the house.

> Thomas's youth was defined more by the advantages afforded him than by the hard times he had to bear — a point often skirted in the telling of his story. His was not the kind of privilege that the wealthy enjoy. What he had were opportunities — nine years of parochial

school education, for example—that most blacks of
his generation in Georgia had to get by without. (Merida
and Fletcher 2007: 55)

In fact, in interviews with many of his elementary and high school
friends, Merida and Fletcher discover that most considered Thomas
to have had more advantages than they did.

> I was like, "When did he live in Pin Point?" The defin-
> ing part of his childhood was anchored in Savannah,
> she knew and it was far from impoverished. "He always
> had money to go to the store to buy ice cream and candy
> [Charlie Mae] Garrett remembered. (Merida and
> Fletcher 2007: 56)

Adding to his privileges, Thomas chose to attend a private, Catholic
boarding school, St. John Vianney, where he was active in a variety of activities, including the newspaper and sports. Though he was
the only African American in his graduating class, he excelled, and
planned on attending seminary and fulfilling his grandfather's dream
by becoming the first Black Catholic priest in Savannah. Immediately after graduating from high school he enrolled in Conception
Seminary in Missouri. He attended Conception for only a year, had
a falling out with his grandfather, and determined to prepare for a
successful life, he enrolled in Holy Cross, a Catholic men's college
near Boston. Thomas' time at Holy Cross has been identified by
his biographers as "radical." (Merida and Fletcher 2007) Though
he faced adversity there as well, which he attributes primarily to
race, Thomas was not only successful at Holy Cross, but his life
changed in other ways as well, as this is where he met his first wife.
Finally, after graduating from Holy Cross, Thomas, now married,
enrolled in Yale Law School. Though there is always debate about
Thomas' abilities, some have argued that Thomas was admitted to
Yale because of an "affirmative action" policy that required that 10
percent of all entering classes in the early 1970s at Yale's famed law
school be minorities. (Merida and Fletcher 2007)

Whether we focus on the incredible educational privileges that
Thomas received—being educated at a top college and a premier
law school—or the contradictions about his early life in Pin Point

and Savannah, some would argue, and we agree, that Thomas' struggles to overcome hardship and adversity, at least to the degree that these are associated with poverty, seem to be exaggerated. Why would Thomas prefer that his story be centered in such a way? Perhaps because Thomas would prefer to think that his struggles were shaped more by social class than by race, thus allowing him to continue to hold racist beliefs himself. This construction of his biography fits into Thomas' ideology of race and allows him to credit his success to two key factors: education and Whites who played a significant role his life, mainly the nuns who taught him at St. Pius.

Evidence for these claims can be found in Thomas' attitudes toward the Black community in Savannah in contrast to his attitudes towards Whites, who were not only products of but also enforcers of Jim Crow segregation.

Though color consciousness is a long-standing issue in the African American community that dates back to the preference—either actual or perceived—that masters and mistresses extended to the sons and daughter that the master conceived—consensually and non-consensually—with his female slaves, Thomas' prejudices against darker-skinned African Americans are deep and profound.

> Aunt Maggie was better educated than most in Pin Point—she could read and write—and she pushed Thomas to learn. She was also light-skinned. Ironically, Thomas would come to dislike Blacks who looked like Aunt Maggie. A string of slights and taunts—some incurred by him as a child, others meted out against his grandfather, Myers Anderson—would harden Thomas against some of the most successful products of his race. To him, most blacks of lighter hue were snobs, the self-appointed superior class of the race who considered themselves a cut above dark-skinned blacks with broad noses and thick lips, like himself. This class-and-color consciousness, not uncommon in the South, would become an obsession with Thomas in his adult life, and that obsession remains with him on the Supreme Court. (Merida and Fletcher 2007: 49)

Not only did Thomas harbor disdain for light-skinned Blacks, but he held Blacks to a higher level of accountability than Whites for causing racial problems. This is evidenced by his incredible patience for Whites who espoused some of the most racist ideologies in our recent history—indeed he not only tolerated but embraced some of the centuries' most ardent segregationists.

> Years after he left Savannah, Thomas would become a loyal Republican, aligning himself with the Strom Thurmonds and Jesse Helmses of the South. And he was willing to cut these former segregationists the kind of slack he wouldn't cut the families of Savannah's black elite.... [referring to Helms] "I have always been taught that on a personal level you judge a person by the way he or she treats the least among us" ... This was the same Jesse Helms who stated in 1979—the year Thomas went to work on Capitol Hill—that segregation wasn't wrong. (Merida and Fletcher 2007: 65)

This willingness to embrace the most outwardly racist of American public figures—Thurmond and Helms—makes understanding Thomas' marriage to Ginny, his second wife, and who is White, particularly interesting. We wonder how Thomas justifies his own interracial marriage when it was outlawed for so many years and would have remained against the law had politicians like Thurmond and Helms had a vote. We ask, how can a judge hate a class of people (light-skinned Blacks) based on his experiences being teased and let that enter into his world view such that it influences his judicial decisions? This question brings us to a discussion of Thomas' decisions as a Supreme Court justice.

Thomas' Professional Life

Across his career as a public servant and especially in the capacity as (a) Director of the Equal Employment Opportunity Commission (EEOC) and (b) Supreme Court Justice, Thomas has earned the reputation of being a staunch, conservative Republican. In his approximately ten-year career as the Chairman (1982 to 1990) of the United States Equal Employment Opportunity Commission (EEOC) Thomas led an office that literally stopped in place the compliance process. (Merida and Fletcher 2007) The backlogs of cases remain today.

Thomas' primary contributions to case law as they are adjudicated in his opinions as a justice on the U.S. Supreme Court have been primarily in cases that hinge on issues of race. He has also weighed in heavily and written important opinions on other areas of inequalities that exist in 21st Century America, specifically, class and gender, including the most recent case addressing bias and retaliation in the workplace. (Greenhouse 2008) Justice Thomas almost always rules against the aggrieved and in favor of corporations or other social institutions (Aka 2006; TerBeek 2006) especially in the two most important posts he has held at the EEOC and as a justice on the U.S. Supreme Court. (Lewis 2007; Williams 1986)

Thomas Reversing *Brown*

Using his position as a U.S. Supreme Court Justice, Thomas has been consistent in his negative votes against promoting integration in public school systems across America and in his insistence that Affirmative Action has no place in American society.

For example, in the school integration case in Seattle, Washington, Justice Thomas vowed that "integration was inherently demeaning to Black children" and based his dissent in the case on the ruling that the U.S. Supreme Court made in *Brown v. Board of Education*, Topeka, Kansas, in 1954.[2] He put it thus:

> The plans before us base school assignment decisions on students' race. Because our Constitution is colorblind, and neither knows nor tolerates classes among citizens, such race-based decision-making is unconstitutional.

---

3. *Brown v. Board of Education* of Topeka, 347 U.S. 483 (1954).

Yet, of course, this is the same "colorblind constitution" that allowed institutionalized segregation through the establishment of Black codes and Jim Crow law, both of which would have limited the types of opportunities Thomas had access to as a young child.

In another example, in the widely debated case of *Grutter v. Bollinger* (02-241) 539 U.S. 306 (2003) 288 F.3d 732, Justice Thomas proffered the major dissent and in so doing squarely cemented himself as a U.S. Supreme Court Justice who, regardless of the terms of the argument, will never offer an opinion that does not differ from his narrow personal beliefs about race relations and justice.

At issue in *Grutter* was the University of Michigan School of Law engaging in admissions policies and practices that were designed to increase the enrollment of underrepresented race/ethnic groups including, but not limited to, African Americans, Hispanics and Native Americans.

Barbara Grutter, a White female Michigan resident applied to the University of Michigan Law School, was wait-listed and subsequently rejected for admission. She filed suit against the institution, charging that the Michigan Law School used discriminatory admissions practices by including race as a 'predominant' factor in its admissions' practices, giving applicants who belong to certain minority groups 'a significantly greater chance of admission than students with similar credentials from privileged racial groups, i.e. Whites. (Aka 2006)

Justice Thomas took grave exception with the majority decision of fellow Justices Sandra Day O'Connor (joined by Souter, Stevens, Ginsburg and Breyer). He charged them with allowing the Michigan Law School to practice unconstitutional racial discrimination. He went on then to quote the great barrister and abolitionist Frederick Douglass this way:

> In regard to the colored people, there is always more that is benevolent, I perceive, than just, manifested towards us. What I ask for the Negro is not benevolence, not pity, not sympathy, but simply *justice*. The American people have always been anxious to know what

they shall do with us.... I have had but one answer from the beginning. Do nothing with us! Your doing with us has already played the mischief with us. Do nothing with us! If the apples will not remain on the tree of their own strength, if they are worm-eaten at the core, if they are early ripe and disposed to fall, let them fall!.... And if the Negro cannot stand on his own legs, let him fall also. All I ask is, give him a chance to stand on his own legs! Let him alone! ... Your interference is doing him positive injury (*Grutter v. Bollinger*, 539 U.S. 306, 349–50 (2003) (*citing* 4 The Frederick Douglass Papers 59, 68.) (J. Blassingame & J. McKivigan eds. 1991)

In furthering his dissent Justice Thomas goes on to state that:

The Constitution does not ... tolerate institutional devotion to the status quo in admissions policies when such devotion ripens into racial discrimination.... No one would argue that a university could set up a lower general admission standard and then impose heightened requirements only on black applicants. Similarly, a university may not maintain a high admissions standard and grant exemptions to favored races." (*Grutter*, 539 U.S. at 350)

Not content to stop there Justice Thomas continues apace "however, because I believe that the Law School's current use of race violates the *Equal Protection Clause* and that the Constitution means the same thing today as it will in 300 months." (*Grutter*, 539 U.S. at 351)

The Thomas dissent in *Grutter* goes down in U.S. social history similarly to the Harlan dissenting opinion in *Plessy v. Ferguson*. Justice Thomas's dissenting opinion in *Grutter* is probably the most "ugly" dissent he has ever delivered. This does not faze Justice Thomas, because, as the *Wall Street Journal* article confirms (Rivkin and Casey 2008), he considers himself an Originalist. This means that Justice Thomas' philosophy is that a judge deciding constitutional issues should confine himself or herself to enforcing norms that are stated or are implicit in the written U.S. Constitution. According to Rivkin and Casey (2008), Justice Thomas' judicial philosophy is as follows:

> I don't put myself in a category. Maybe I am labeled as an originalist or something, but it's not my constitution to play around with. Let's just start with that. We're citizens. It's our country, it's our constitution. I don't feel I have any particular right to put my gloss on your constitution. My job is simply to interpret it.

Another example of Thomas' position on school integration and affirmative action comes in the recent case involving the Seattle Public schools. His opinion in this case—one of two decided in the summer of 2007, both of which significantly turned back the school integration gains made by Brown—makes it very plain what his individualistic beliefs are all about when it comes to school integration policies. He put it thus:

> What was wrong in 1954 cannot be right today. Whatever else the Court's rejection of the segregationists' arguments in Brown might have established, it certainly made clear that state and local governments cannot take from the Constitution a right to make decisions on the basis of race by adverse possession ... None of the considerations trumpeted by the dissent is relevant to the constitutionality of the school boards' race-based plans because no contextual detail—or collection of contextual details, post, at 2–22—can "provide refuge from the principle that under our Constitution, the government may not make distinctions on the basis of race." Adarand, 515 U.S., at 240, 115 S. Ct. 2097, 132 L. Ed. 2d 158 (THOMAS, J., concurring in part and concurring in judgment) ... It is the height of arrogance for Members of this Court to assert blindly that their motives are better than others ... As a matter of social experimentation, the laws in question must satisfy the requirements of the Constitution. While this Court has permitted the States to legislate or otherwise officially act

experimentally in the social and economic fields, it has always recognized and held that this power is subject to the limitations of the Constitution, and that the tests of the Constitution must be met"); In place of the color-blind Constitution, the dissent would permit measures to keep the races together and proscribe measures to keep the races apart ... But in view of the Constitution, in the eye of the law, there is in this country no superior, dominant, ruling class of citizens.... Our Constitution is color-blind, and neither knows nor tolerates classes among citizens"). Indeed, if our history has taught us anything, it has taught us to beware of elites bearing racial theories.... Can we really be sure that the racial theories that motivated Dred Scott and Plessy are a relic of the past or that future theories will be nothing but beneficent and progressive? That is a gamble I am unwilling to take, and it is one the Constitution does not allow ... Indeed, the racial theories endorsed by the Seattle school board should cause the dissenters to question whether local school boards should be entrusted with the power to make decisions on the basis of race Plessy, supra, at 559, 16 S. Ct. 1138, 41 L. Ed. 256 (Harlan, J., dissenting). I concur in THE CHIEF JUSTICE's opinion so holding.[3]

His biographers—Merida and Fletcher—argue that Thomas' opposition to integration, especially school integration, is rooted in his experiences with segregated and integrated education as a young man.

---

4. (*Parents Involved in Community Schools, Petitioner v. Seattle School District No. 1 et al.; Crystal D. Meredith, Custodial Parent and Next Friend of Joshua Ryan McDonald, Petitioner v. Jefferson County Board of Education et al.* Nos. 05-908 and 05-915 Supreme Court of the United States 127 S. Ct. 2738; 168 L. Ed. 2d 508; 2007 U.S. LEXIS 8670; 75 U.S.L.W. 4577; 20 Fla. L. Weekly Fed. S 490 June 28, 2007, * Decided (145–150).

Thomas would later reflect on his time at St. Pius with a mixture of anger and remorse. The school, which opened in 1952 and closed in 1971, became a casualty of integration ... In outlining the benefits of Pius's closure, the headmaster of Benedictine, one of the White schools, explained, "that in America today, quality education includes the growth in knowledge and maturity that can only come when people whose lives are oriented by the same spiritual and moral values are able to share them with one another. Such sharing, of course, is not possible when they are kept apart by such artificial barriers as the color of their skins ..."As a practicing Catholic, Thomas would find it difficult to disagree with that ideal. But he would spend his career battling such logic as it related to education. Even though he didn't graduate from Pius, its closure—and the closure of other black Catholic schools—helped sour him forever on integration. (Merida and Fletcher 2007: 67)

Thomas would go on to say: "Some people think that the solution to all the problems of Black people is integration. I never worshiped at the altar [of integration] ... The poor education for Blacks that resulted from some of these decisions deeply saddens me. It was very harmful." (Merida and Fletcher 2007: 67)

Additionally, as mentioned earlier, Justice Thomas sees himself as a staunch Originalist. What of course is interesting in Thomas' adherence to this ideological position is that the U.S. Constitution, in its original form, did not recognize people of African descent as human beings. As recently as the Dred Scot decision of 1858, the court ruled that people of African descent constituted just 3/5ths of a human being. (Hattery and Smith 2007b) The inherent contradiction between Thomas' ideological position as an originalist and his lived reality as an African American is striking and indeed stunning.

Thomas' position is also provocative in its contradiction to the wealth of social scientific evidence demonstrating the impact of more than 400 years of structured, institutionalized racism (Bonilla-Silva 2004; Feagin 1991), which has blocked access to housing, education, occupations, church membership, country club membership, and virtually every aspect of political, economic and social life. (Hattery and Smith 2007a; Hattery and Smith 2006) And, as a child born into the Jim Crow South, Thomas certainly would have experienced these forms of institutionalized racism. This disconnect then provides the point of departure for our examination of his personal life.

Thomas' Intimate Relationships

Thomas has been married twice. He met his first wife, Kathy Ambush, during his junior year at Holy Cross. Kathy was a student at nearby Anna Maria College. After dating for a week, Thomas declared that he was "in love." Some have suggested that his relationship with Kathy was a major reason for him to stay enrolled at Holy Cross despite how difficult it was. Kathy, who is African American, grew up in what Thomas' biographers describe as a " ... loving, stable, socially conscious family ..." that was welcoming to Thomas. In many ways, Kathy's family provided the loving home that Thomas never had. (Merida and Fletcher 2007) Thomas and Kathy were married the day after he graduated from Holy Cross— June 5, 1971. In 1973, while Thomas was at Yale Law School, their only son Jamal was born, and he and Kathy divorced a decade later in 1984, several years after their separation in 1981. As part of the settlement agreement, Thomas agreed to take full custody of Jamal and raise him. Jamal, now in his mid-thirties, is an investment banker with Wachovia, a position that requires Thomas to recuse himself from all cases involving Wachovia. (Mauro 2007)

Biographers of Thomas note that the marriage had been in decline for many years, based primarily on the diverging interests of Kathy and Clarence:

> The breakup of the marriage appears to have been by
> mutual desire. Their 'mismatch of ambition,' as one
> friend had put it, became accentuated as their political

views diverged and Kathy pursued a career. (Thomas
2002: 251)

Only a few short years later, Thomas met Virginia (Ginni) Lamp,
a White woman who had worked in various posts for the Republican Party in Washington, D.C. Thomas and Ginni met in 1986 at
an Anti-Defamation League conference. They dated for a year and
were married on May 30, 1987, in Omaha, Nebraska. Thomas' son,
Jamal, served as Thomas' best man.

Thomas' intimate relationships pose some interesting questions
for the scholar or student of interracial intimacies. On the one
hand, like Frederick Douglass, Thomas has married women on
both sides of the color line. Yet, whereas Douglass' marriage to
Helen Pitts was described by both as an attempt to "walk the walk"
when it came to race relations, the battle for racial equality, and
integration, Thomas' marriage to Ginni is interpreted by some as
an abandonment of his race. Or, perhaps it is an attempt on his
part to transcend the conventional categories of race. Or, perhaps
it is based in his rejection of Blacks, particularly dark-skinned Blacks
and his preference for being around Whites, even those with conservative attitudes on race, which, ironically, are similar to his own
perspectives on race.

Friends of Thomas note that before he met Ginni, Thomas made
it widely known that he found "… Black women in DC [were] so difficult." (Merida and Fletcher 2007: 166) Though he was named by
Jet as one of Washington's most eligible bachelors, Thomas attributed his inability to get a date with a Black woman to the fact that
he worked for Ronald Reagan, which Thomas claimed was like wearing a "scarlet letter." (Merida and Fletcher 2007:166) He is quoted:

> "This is a rough town," he told a Black conservative
> friend. "Can't get no pussy out here from these [Black]
> women." (Merida and Fletcher 2007: 167)

Perhaps Thomas conceded that given his very conservative far right
ideologies that he would struggle to find a Black woman who would
tolerate those views and he would be better off pursuing a relationship with a White woman.

What's interesting, of course, is that Thomas's interracial marriage is to a conservative, Republican woman, a group not necessarily known for being progressive on race issues. One of the ways that it seems that his wife and her family have of dealing with this cognitive dissonance is by minimizing Thomas' "Blackness."

One interesting and perplexing issue is the seemingly contradictory construction of Thomas' racial identity by both Thomas and his wife, Ginni. Speaking explicitly about race, Ginni is quoted as saying:

> I don't see my husband as Black. I've never put up barriers in my life that don't make sense. When we met, I was so drawn to his integrity, his values, his intelligence. (Noonan 1997)

Ginni's family, it is reported, also had some concerns about their interracial relationship, but like Ginni, they deal with this in part by minimizing Thomas' "Blackness."

> "But he was so nice, we forgot he was Black," said Ginni's aunt Opal from Iowa, "and he treated her so well, all of his other qualities made up for his being Black." (Merida and Fletcher 2007: 165)

Ginni's and her family's dismissal or minimization of Thomas' racial identity is starkly contrasted with his own views about himself. As noted previously, biographers of Thomas provide many examples, as we cite above, of Thomas' acknowledgement of his "negroid" features and his disgust of these traits. Yet he is in constant tension with the Black community and despite his features, feels it necessary to reinforce his racial identity, especially in the face of critiques by prominent African Americans, including Al Sharpton, that Thomas is an "Uncle Tom," or not really "Black." In an interview in 1984, Thomas is quoted as saying: "What offends me is the civil rights community saying I'm not Black." (Merida and Fletcher 2007: 164)

To further complicate matters of race in Thomas' personal life, Thomas and Ginni are the legal guardians to Thomas' great-nephew,

Marky. Marky's father, Thomas' sister's son, is serving a lengthy sentence in prison for drug trafficking and Marky's mother, a White woman, is simply too overwhelmed to raise four children on her own. In January of 1998, Thomas and Ginni were awarded legal custody of Marky and they have been raising him as their son ever since.

Most of Thomas' friends and associates note the incredible changes that a second round of fatherhood has played in Thomas' life. He is known to re-arrange his court schedule so that he can pick up Marky after school and his and Ginni's social life revolves around spending time with Marky. Clearly, most agree that this decision has been good for all involved. (Merida and Fletcher 2007) We wonder, given the fact that Thomas has several nieces and nephews that need assistance, why he and Ginni chose only to take legal and physical custody of Marky. Perhaps it is because Marky's bi-racial background makes him "blend in" better in Thomas' interracial family.

Conclusion

Clarence Thomas has, in many ways, the complex personal and professional life that characterizes the contemporary United States and its continued struggle with race relations. Thomas is, by any definition, a successful African American man and one of the rare individuals of any race or gender to occupy such a lofty status as to sit as a justice on the U.S. Supreme Court. He is in an interracial marriage and is raising a bi-racial relative. Despite these complexities in his personal life, his public musings about race are quite conservative and some argue that he has disdain for both light-skinned African Americans — of similar complexion as his great nephew whom he is raising — and for African Americans who, like him, have what he terms "negroid" features. Professionally, during any given court cycle he sits in judgment of national policies that address race relations in the U.S., including some highly charged school integration cases. Certainly it is not our position to challenge or judge Thomas' life nor his decision, but we do wonder about how Thomas reconciles all of his feelings about race and the decisions he makes as a supreme court justice with the complexities of his personal life. We also wonder, as with Jefferson and Thurmond, about the prudence in being allowed by the privileges associated with one's status, to enter one's personal ideologies about race and interracial relationships — ideologies that are often damaging to African Americans — into the public discourse and in the case of Thomas, into the laws that govern such important aspects of the lives of Americans as education. It certainly seems that the U.S. Supreme Court is no more a place than the office of the President nor the U.S. Senate for an individual such as Thomas to work out the contradictions around race and intimacy that he lives in his personal life.

Chapter Eight

William and Janet Langhart Cohen: Love in Black and White

Curiously, while I anticipated that black people might hold some measure of hostility for me being The Man who stepped into their garden and picked one of their most beautiful flowers, their reaction has been just the opposite. They understand that I chose to cross the color line, not as a display of power, but because of the power of love for a woman who happened to be one of them. (Cohen and Cohen 2007: 277–79)

Introduction

The story of William Cohen and Janet Langhart Cohen is unlike any of the others in this book, primarily because unlike the other stories we have explored and examined, Cohen has spent a great deal of time reflecting on his marriage, which crosses lines of both race and religion. His writings on race and interracial relationships are much more extensive than any of the other cases we have researched and discussed. Thus, the challenge in this chapter is to boil down his very thorough and self-reflective analysis in a way that allows the reader to glimpse this relationship in much the same way that he or she has glimpsed the relationships of others, such as Clarence Thomas and Thomas Jefferson. Perhaps the biggest difference in our analysis of the relationship between William Cohen and Janet Langhart Cohen is the fact that Janet has written her own memoir and collaborated with William on this public accounting of their relationship. The vast majority of women in the relationships we have explored have been silent, often because they were illiterate or so lacking in power and privilege that they had no access point to enter the public discourse. The account provided by Janet Langhart Cohen provides the voice we wish we could give to Sally Hemings or Julia Chin, whose stories would no doubt have expanded our understanding of interracial couplings in the social, political and economic landscape of the United States in which they lived.

Early Life—William Cohen

William Cohen was born in Bangor, Maine, on August 28, 1940. William's introduction to crossing heavily patrolled lines of demarcation began the moment he was born to an Irish Catholic mother and a Jewish father. William's grandfather was seriously opposed to his son marrying a "gentile," so much so that his parents hid their marriage until his mother was pregnant with him. Though his parents built a comfortable middle-class life through their mom-and-pop business—their bakery provided the bread for local households and restaurants across Bangor—William's experiences with religion were complex and critical in forming his attitudes towards those different from him.

William's mother was Irish Catholic but for a variety of reasons was never invested in organized religion and did not attend church either as a child or an adult. "Irish Catholic" was more of an ethnic than religious identity in Cohen's family. Similarly, though Cohen's father was Jewish, his attendance at the temple was complicated by issues of social class and he limited his attendance primarily to high holidays. That said, like many other "identities," being Jewish transcends one's practice of the religion. Partly in an attempt to lay claim to the Jewish identity his father felt he lost when he married an Irish Catholic woman, and in part to repair the relationship with Cohen's grandfather, his father decided that William would attend Hebrew school and prepare for his bar mitzvah. Although there were many life-altering experiences in William's early life, this was perhaps the most potent in shaping his attitudes and beliefs about inclusion and exclusion.

Most Americans have at lease a brief image of William Cohen in their heads because he has appeared on television consistently for the last 30 years, first in his role as a United States Senator (Maine) and then as Secretary of Defense. Admittedly, we had never considered how William's appearance shaped his experience as a Jew in Bangor, Maine. Physically, William favors his mother: his coloring is fair. When he joined other young Jewish boys at Hebrew school, they treated him as a pariah, an outsider, claiming—largely on his looks rather than his ancestry—that he was not really Jewish. His exclusion from the Jewish community culminated in his final year at Hebrew school. In a mandatory meeting with the rabbi in preparation for his Bar Mitzvah, William was informed that because his mother was not Jewish, additional rituals would have to be performed before he could transition to full, adult membership in the Jewish temple. Namely, either his mother would have to convert—which William was sure would never happen given his mother's distaste for organized religion—or he would have to undergo a conversion ceremony himself that involved having a drop of blood drawn from his penis. Outraged, William left the temple and never returned.

William's experience with Hebrew school clearly shaped not only his beliefs about religion—he would never actively participate in organized religion again—but it also provided him a potent experience with discrimination. He was discriminated against by Christians, both adults and peers, for being Jewish and he was ostracized from the Jewish community for not being Jewish enough. These powerful experiences in his youth strongly shaped William's understanding of prejudice and discrimination, and probably opened his mind to the point where he would be willing to pursue an interracial relationship in his adult life.

In addition to his personal experiences with prejudice and anti-Semitism, William also witnessed firsthand the horror of racism in the 1960s American landscape. One such experience occurred when William was in college. Between 1958 and 1962 he attended and graduated from Bowdoin College in Maine. He was the star of their basketball team. An all-men's school at the time, they did admit African Americans, though the population on campus reflected the Black population in Maine: it was tiny. Among his classmates was a young African American man who also played on the basketball team. One evening during their junior year, the two attempted to hitchhike to a nearby town for some fun. Though his friend, Ed, knew immediately what the problem was, William was perplexed by the fact that no drivers would stop to pick them up. This contradicted his many previous experiences with hitchhiking in rural Maine. On Ed's recommendation, Ed hid in the bushes while William stood alone thumbing a ride. Immediately drivers stopped, but none would carry both William and Ed. Not willing to leave his friend alone, they walked along the road, drank some whiskey they had brought along with them, and proceeded to get drunk and fall asleep in the bushes. Shortly after, someone called the police who arrived to see what the trouble was. Upon encountering William and Ed, they sent William on his way and insisted on arresting Ed. William followed his friend to jail and called his mother, who bailed Ed out. This experience of differential treatment, especially by the police, would permanently shape William's racial attitudes, approach to public policy, and personal life.

Early Life — Janet Langhart

Janet Langhart was born Janet Leola Floyd, December 22, 1941, in Indianapolis, Indiana. Though Indianapolis is certainly not the Deep South (see Hattery & Smith 2006), Indiana has a long and sordid history of racism: the Ku Klux Klan has many very large and active chapters in Indiana and one of the last "official" lynchings in the U.S. took place in southern Indiana in the late 1930s. Janet's youth was characterized by the same strict rules of Jim Crow segregation that dominated social relations across the "official" South — south of the Mason-Dixon line.

Janet's parents met in early 1941 and by the spring they were involved in a whirlwind dating relationship that included dining in restaurants and going to dances on base (Janet's father—Sewell Bridges—was in the army and served as one of the "Black Panthers," the first "Negro" tank unit in the United States army). In the spring of 1941, her mother became pregnant and before she and Janet's father could marry he was re-deployed to Europe to fight in WWII. While still pregnant, Janet's mother married another boyfriend, Russell Floyd, who was very much in love with Janet's mother and insisted only that they raise Janet as his daughter and that her true father never be revealed. Thus, Janet was born "Janet Floyd." Interestingly, the doctor who delivered Janet bungled her name—Janet's mother had intended to name her "Jeannette"—and also her race: he marked the "White" box on her birth certificate. This early act was prophetic in signaling Janet's struggles with race and racial identity.

Her mother's marriage to Russell Floyd broke up by the time Janet was three years old and she and her mother embarked on the life characterized by being a female-headed household. On their own, in the mid-1940s in segregated Indianapolis, Janet's early life was characterized by struggle, especially on the part of her mother. Like the majority of African American women of this time, Janet's mother found steady work as a domestic—cooking and cleaning for White families (see Hill Collins 1994 and Segura 1994). She worked for many different families across Janet's childhood and several of these families were Jewish. Many years later, when Janet would finally meet William's father, she would remark that their conversations, which often centered on food, were indicative of an interesting fact: having grown up eating "Jewish food" that her mother cooked for the families for whom she worked and then often brought home—as leftovers—from work, Janet knew more about Jewish food than William!

Janet's mother was typical of African American women who worked as domestics during the 20th century: there was always food for her family, but her wages were meager and often they "lived in" with the families for whom she worked (Rollins 1985). Thus, in contrast to William's childhood, during which he had very little exposure to African Americans, Janet had a great deal of exposure to Whites. Yet, as we argue elsewhere (Hattery & Smith 2007; Smith

& Hattery 2009), Jim Crow-style segregation was instituted *precisely* to create social distance among "the races" who were otherwise in close, intimate contact. Typical of most Southern African Americans of the mid-20th century, Janet was around Whites all the time, but racial attitudes and patterns of segregation meant that she was never allowed to develop any type of true relationship that crossed racial lines.

Though it is impossible to paint one picture of the African American experience in the mid-South in the middle of the 20th century, in many ways Janet's experience was "typical." Her life was determined by patterns of segregation: she attended racially segregated schools and churches, and lived in racially segregated neighborhoods. Janet remarked that one of the experiences that most profoundly shaped her was the 1955 lynching of Emmett Till, a 14-year-old Chicago boy who was shot in the head after being brutally beaten, his body tied to a cotton gin fan and thrown in the Tallahatchie River, after he allegedly whistled at a White woman in Money, Mississippi. Janet and Emmett were the same age. This historical event, along with others, including witnessing a cross-burning, watching a Klan parade pass her home, learning of her father's mistreatment when he returned to the United States after liberating a concentration camp in Europe during WWII, and the lynching of her own cousin, forever shaped Janet's racial consciousness and political ideology. (Langhart Cohen 2004; Cohen 2007)

Professional Life — William Cohen

William's college experience was not an easy road. He struggled academically, in part because of his involvement in sports and social life, particularly fraternity life. Finally, in his senior year, he found his intellectual stride and graduated from Bowdoin (Brunswick, Maine) well enough prepared to pursue a career in law. William was admitted to Boston University School of Law and began his studies in the fall of 1962. In reflecting on his time in law school, he notes that it was incredibly challenging, but it also exposed him to some of the best legal minds in the country as well as to successful politicians. After he graduated from law school, he moved back to Maine, where he dabbled in private practice for a short time before eventually serving as the county district attorney. It was this experience that turned William on to politics. He began his political career at the local level, serving simultaneously on the city council and school board of Bangor. Comparing the law to politics, it was evident to William early on that his talents clearly lay in politics. Others soon recognized William for his abilities as an administrator and he was catapulted first into state politics and shortly thereafter into national politics. After walking hundreds of miles across the state of Maine to drum up support for his candidacy, William Cohen ran his first successful national campaign and was elected to the U.S. House of Representatives in 1972.

William's political career would be characterized by two core traits: his commitment to bi-partisanship and his maverick style, and both would become evident in his first term. William's political career was primarily set in motion by the leading crisis of the time: Watergate. As a new Republican on Capitol Hill, his colleagues would look to him for support for Richard Nixon. As a "freshman" Congressman, Cohen would break with his own party and argue and vote for the impeachment of President Nixon. He would argue, twenty-five years later, that though he was troubled by President Clinton's sexual liaison with Monica Lewinsky (William was Clinton's secretary of defense at the time), that Clinton's conduct did not threaten the U.S. Constitution in nearly the same magnitude as had Nixon's. After three terms in the House of Representatives, William ran for and was elected to the U.S. Senate in 1978. As was the case in the House of Representatives, William's career in the Senate was marked by his commitment to bi-partisanship and "getting it right," and his willingness to break with his party. Most notably, William's career in the Senate was built around his involvement on the Armed Services Committee. His service on the Armed Services Committee exposed William to the role that the United States played in international politics vis a vis the military. In particular, William used this opportunity to become an expert on foreign policy.

After twelve years of serving in the U.S. Senate, and having made the decision to retire from public service, William was called on by President Clinton to serve as the Secretary of Defense. William's twelve years on the Armed Services Committee prepared him well for this role, yet his appointment to this inner cabinet post was highly controversial because it crossed party lines. William served in this capacity from 1997 to 2001, overseeing such controversial events as the U.S. bombings in Iraq and Kosovo, the first Gulf War, and the terrorist bombings of the U.S. embassies in Tanzania and Kenya. After standing in public service for 30 years, William Cohen retired as Secretary of Defense at the end of the Clinton administration in 2001.

Though William's public career is not filled with decisions that are explicitly about race, his career is filled with examples of working in a truly bi-partisan manner, including as a Republican in President Clinton's inner cabinet, which clearly came about because of William's ability to see across well-entrenched lines of demarcation. We argue that many of William's experiences as a child, living in two different worlds—alienated by both Jews and Christians, for example—developed in him an ability to see himself and define his life outside of traditional boxes. This definition of himself created opportunities in his professional life that depended upon just this ability. And, as we will argue in the final section of this chapter, these experiences set the stage for his personal and romantic life, as well.

Professional Life—Janet Langhart Cohen

Janet's mother had high hopes for her daughter, wishing, among other things, that Janet would one day perform as a pianist in Carnegie Hall. Though this has not yet happened, Janet's mother's high expectations inculcated in Janet a pattern of setting high expectations for herself and establishing a work ethic that allowed her to achieve her goals.

Janet knew that one key to achieving her goals would be education. She worked hard in high school and despite having attended a segregated Indianapolis, Indiana, high school—Crispus Atticus, which is probably best known for college and NBA basketball Hall of Famer Oscar Robertson, one of Janet's classmates—which was under-resourced in comparison to the schools White students attended, she was admitted to Butler University—a predominately White university—in Indianapolis. Janet spent two years at Butler before leaving to pursue a career in modeling; a decision that would prove to be both fortuitous and painful—not only did this opportunity expose Janet to powerful African Americans, but it also exposed Janet to more of the hurt of segregation. As a model, Janet traveled the United States, which exposed her to more experiences with Jim Crow segregation—Black models were forced to stay in inferior accommodations—but it also exposed her to some of the most influential African Americans of the time, including Martin Luther King, Mahalia Jackson, and Bob Johnson. As a model, Janet developed skills and made connections that would lead to opportunities in the broadcast media: namely in television.

Janet began her broadcasting career in Chicago, where in 1969 she was offered the opportunity to be the "weathergirl" for a UHF station that presented "A Black View of the News." (Cohen 2007:175) One can easily argue that she paved the way for the most famous Black woman in television, who also happens to broadcast from Chicago: Oprah Winfrey. Janet was also involved in breaking other color barriers, including being the first African American woman to be allowed to try on clothes in Marshall Fields. Fields, the landmark retail store in Chicago, enforced Jim Crow codes that prohibited African Americans from trying on clothes in the store—a pattern that was typical all through the South. As part of her role as a model for Marshall Fields, she was allowed not only to change clothes in the dressing room, but even to model wedding dresses—something that had never before been allowed for African American women.

Janet's on-air experience and her exposure as a model—she appeared on the cover of JET several times—opened up other doors of opportunity. In 1973, she had her own daily talk show in Indianapolis called "Indy Today with Janet Langhart." (Cohen 2007; 175) By 1974 she had accepted a job as a co-host on a daily show in Boston, and this is where she and William first met. For the next 30 years, Janet appeared on many different broadcasts in Boston, Chicago, and New York. She worked for programs including "Entertainment Tonight" (ET) and did several special assignments for ABC and BET. Among her many contributions, some would argue that it was in her position as "First Lady of the Pentagon" that Janet had her greatest impact. In this role she facilitated the first real conversations between service members, their families, and Pentagon officials. She also spearheaded the development of a series of initiatives designed to address morale among both the troops and the Pentagon staff. Finally, Janet has worked tirelessly with supporters in the U.S. Senate to orchestrate an official apology by the United States government for the tens of thousands of lynchings of African Americans in the late 19th and early 20th centuries.

Most recently she has explored her experiences with race in her memoir *My Life in Two Americas* (2004) and a one-act play *Anne and Emmett*—which appears as an appendix in her book with her husband—that employs a fictional conversation between Anne Frank and Emmett Till to explore the universality of hate.

Romantic Relationships

Both William and Janet had previous relationships before they began dating each other in the early 1990s. William married his first wife, Diane Dunn, shortly before he graduated from Bowdoin in 1962. He and Diane had two children together. Though on the surface it might seem that William and Diane had more in common— she is White and also grew up in Maine—their ambitions, aspirations, and world views were not shared and ultimately his commitment first to law and second to politics coupled with his extensive travel schedule led to their divorce.

Janet had also been married, twice, before marrying William. She was married very briefly to Melvin Anthony Langhart followed by an 11-year marriage to Robert Kistner, a distinguished Harvard Medical School professor, who is White. Thus, for Janet, unlike for

William, the decision to marry across the color line was a barrier she crossed before she and William decided to marry. But, that does not mean that Janet's family responded warmly to her decisions to marry outside her race.

Janet had been raised with very clear messages about Whites: they were not to be trusted. Janet recalled one day when she was young and her aunt Leola came home with a White baby she was caring for.

> She laid the baby down on the couch to nap. I saw the baby and was mesmerized by her sparkling, blue eyes. I stepped closer to get a better view. The baby started to whimper and reach out to me, signaling that she wanted me to pick her up. I lifted the baby up and cradled her in my arms. Just then Aunt Leola stormed into the room. "Put *that thing* down," she shouted. "Don't start to feel anything for that thing because as soon as she grows up from looking like your little baby doll she's going to call you a nigger." (Cohen 2007:44)

The message was loud and clear: don't get emotionally invested in White people. Why? Because they are the people who owned your great-grandparents. Because they forced your great-grandmothers to have sex with them and bear mulatto children and then with their breasts full, were forced to suckle the mistress's children. This practice continued long into the 20th century as Whites preferred Black women as wet nurses while simultaneously enforcing strict rules of segregation on drinking fountains—a perplexing contradiction. (See Hattery & Smith 2009.)

When Janet briefly dated a White peer at Butler, her mother remarked "Remember, no matter how many times you cross the color line, this side is home. You can dance and play over there, but when the music stops, he'll go home. It's us, your people, that you'll always have to come back to. They'll never accept you as an equal." (Cohen 2007: 277)

Janet's mother's concern is not atypical; in fact it is captured in the incredibly popular play *Fiddler on the Roof*. Tevye—the father in *Fiddler on the Roof*—proclaims that: "As the good book says

'Each shall seek his own kind.' In other words, a bird may love a fish but where would they build a home together?"

Though Janet's marriage to Dr. Kistner prepared her family for marriages that crossed both racial and religious lines—Dr. Kistner was Catholic—the marriage ended very traumatically with Dr. Kistner, depressed by the reality that aging caused his skills as a surgeon to deteriorate to the point that he could no longer practice, he committed suicide. A very nasty legal battle over his inheritance ensued, that interestingly enough turned on Janet's race. Kistner's estate attorney remarked, in front of Janet's counsel—F. Lee Bailey—and several other people who were present: "The Black bitch got more than she deserves. She got the pleasure of being with Dr. Kistner, and she's not entitled to a damn thing. She's gotten all she's going to get. I took the case to make sure of that." (Cohen 2007: 256)

Not long after Kistner's suicide, William contacted Janet and invited her to attend a Broadway play with him. Their first date ended with William confessing his love for Janet and thus began their long courtship.

In contrast to Janet's experience growing up with negative messages about Whites, William's experience is typical of Whites raised in the North: little personal contact with Blacks. Furthermore, as a member of the dominant culture, one can argue that William's parents were required to spend less time—perhaps no time at all—teaching lessons about race precisely because the lessons of privilege and domination are so widely available in the dominant ideology of race and race relations that there is less duty on the part of parents who hold these beliefs—or at a minimum don't resist them—to reinforce them with their children.

Interestingly, William titles the chapter in which he writes about bringing Janet home to meet his parents "Guess Who's Coming to Dinner," a reference to the Kathryn Hepburn-Sidney Poitier Academy Awarding winning film by the same name. William was certain that his parents would grow to accept Janet and love her as their daughter-in-law, but he was also aware that they had lived their whole lives in the segregated, White north. "While I had never heard either my father or mother utter a racial slur, they had had absolutely zero contact with Black people during the course of their lives." (Cohen 2007: 273) William's parents didn't blink when he arrived on their doorstep with Janet. They immediately embraced her and they had a comfortable and supportive relationship.

> Janet's race did not present any problem for them. For example, one day a gossip magazine called my father while he was at work to seek his reaction to my romance "with a Black woman." Apparently, the mixing machines were roaring at the time and the question had to be repeated several times. The reporter, in exasperation, practically shouted the words "BLACK WOMAN!" Dad, thinking the reporter was trying to provoke a negative reaction from him, shouted back, "SHE'S NOT THAT BLACK!" and slammed the receiver down. He knew nothing of the perverse notion of color coding but simply had lived at a time when Black people were called "colored." He had concluded that the reporter, in calling Janet a Black woman, was insinuating a negative: that she was not worthy of his son's affection or approval. (Cohen 2007: 275)

Courtship and Marriage

William and Janet's courtship and marriage were perhaps shaped less by their race and religious differences than by their occupations. For example, though many interracial couples receive harsh or disparaging looks when they are out in public—at restaurants, the movies or the mall—William's very public life as a U.S. Senator and Janet's recognizable face earned as a model and television talk-show host, seemed to have given others the false impression that they had some entitlement to comment on William and Janet's relationship. William writes about the many instances from having dinner in their favorite Italian restaurant to attending Washington Wizards basketball games when people felt entitled and apparently compelled to make audible comments about William and Janet's relationship. Often the comments were positive, especially from

African American men who expressed camaraderie with William for dating "a sister," but often the comments were negative, like the reporter who called William's father; people often worried about the message that was being conveyed when a White man of William's stature had chosen to love and commit his life to an African American woman.

Internally, William and Janet's relationship moved along like most others, with their biggest barrier being their schedules. The life of a U.S. Senator involves a great deal of travel, and William's position on the Armed Forces committee exacerbated that. Additionally, Janet's work on televisions specials often took her to remote and exotic locations around the world. Making *time* to pursue a relationship was perhaps their biggest challenge.

William and Janet dated for about four years before they were married, though William writes that he fell in love with Janet on their first date and both he and Janet point out almost prophetically their chance meeting twenty years before their first date. William believes it was serendipitous whereas Janet believes it was destiny. Either way, they found their way into each other's lives and the only thing that kept them from marrying earlier was that Janet frequently remarked that she didn't want to be married to a politician. For a variety of reasons, primarily being burned out from his work, William decided after three terms in the Senate, that he would not seek re-election. Anticipating that he would seek Janet's hand in marriage after his retirement from the Senate, "Much as Janet and I loved each other, I'm not sure our wedding would have arrived as soon but for her accidental encounter with a dog that had been either lost or abandoned." (Cohen 2007: 291) That chance encounter led to Janet adopting the dog in an the spur of the moment only to realize after signing the papers that she had just signed a new lease on a condo in Washington that prohibited animals! Desperate, she and Lucky—the dog—arrived on William's doorstep and to quote a colloquial phrase, "the rest is history."

This moment generated in William a sense of urgency, of "if not now, when?" and William and Janet were married a few months later in the Capitol building on Valentine's Day in 1996. Ten years later, and after having survived the pressures of William's four years as the Secretary of Defense for President Bill Clinton, William and Janet remain committed to each other and to the work of racial reconciliation.

Conclusion

The relationship between William and Janet Langhart Cohen, though perhaps relatively common among interracial relationships in the United States, is unusual when compared to the others detailed in this book. How? Of all the interracial relationships we have explored in this book, the Cohen's is the only relationship between a White man and an African American woman that is *purely* consensual. There are, no doubt, many interracial relationships between White men and African American women that are healthy and strong. Yet, the interracial relationships between White men *in positions of political power* and African American women — that are detailed in this book — are most often based on tremendous power differentials that render them structurally or effectively unequal — Thomas Jefferson owns Sally Hemings, Strom Thurmond alone dictates the terms of his relationship with both his mistress (Carrie Butler) and his daughter (Essie Mae Washington). And, certainly in terms of the structural power that is embedded in systems of patriarchy and racial domination, William Cohen has access to institutionalized power that Janet Langhart Cohen does not. That said, William's relationship with Janet is not built principally on the same types of structural and institutionalized power that the majority we've researched for this book have been. Unlike Thomas Jefferson, William does not own Janet; unlike Strom Thurmond, William does not inhabit a world so structured by institutionalized segregation that he is unwilling to resist social norms in order to live as a "family" with his mistress and their daughter; unlike Richard Mentor Johnson, William can be — and is — legally married to his love partner. This difference in the Cohen's relationship stands in stark contrast to the majority of this configuration that have existed among men of political power across U.S. history.

Another key difference between the Cohens' relationship and so many others that we researched for this book is that William and Janet have open and very honest discussions about race, race relations, religion and other contentious issues that plague the American landscape. And, this is not simply a reflection of the Cohens' being a contemporary relationship. For example, in researching the relationship between Clarence and Virginia Thomas, his biographers reveal that the Thomases deal with race at the most basic level they are required to, but that they do not have protracted discussions about systems of domination—including racial domination—that plague the United States generally and proscribe the parameters of individual interracial relationships. In contrast, the Cohens deal with issues of race, religion and social class—among other things—in a straightforward and honest manner that recognizes both their differences in individual experiences and their embeddedness in a social structure.

Finally, it is clear, especially from researching the more contemporary couples we write about in this book, that William and Janet's interest in and commitment to each other and to racial reconciliation is based in their shared experiences with discrimination and oppression. Janet's play *Anne and Emmett*[1] explores the universality of hate through the eyes of two young teenagers who were murdered out of hate, but in many ways it is also a reflection of the conversations William and Janet have had about their own experiences as victims or witnesses to racial and religious oppression and exploitation.

---

1. For more information on Janet's play *Anne and Emmett* visit the website: http://www.anneandemmett.com/.

Chapter Nine

Strom Thurmond, Segregationist and Father of a "Black" Daughter

On the question of social intermingling of the races, our people draw the line. All the laws of Washington and all the bayonets of the army cannot force the Negro race into our theatres, our swimming pools, our schools, our churches and our homes.

Strom Thurmond,
speech at the Dixiecrat Convention, 1948

Introduction

Of all the individuals whose lives we have explored in this book, Strom Thurmond's is perhaps the most intriguing, for two reasons: (1) his life spans the entire 20th century—a period over which the United States struggled as violently and vehemently as ever about its racial history—and because (2) Thurmond was written about extensively by experts, but it is the memoir of his "Black" daughter, Essie Mae Washington-Williams, that allows us not only a different window on his life, but also a lens that often differs distinctly from that offered by the historians, political scientists, and journalists who describe his life.

Early Life

To examine Thurmond's public life is to explore the power of race to shape politics, to see first the unques-

tioned acceptance of segregation, then the fierce resistance to any challenge to "custom and tradition," that
deceptively benign euphemism, and finally to witness the
accommodations that were required when southern
blacks stepped forward to claim their place in southern
political life. (Cohodas 1993: 12)

Strom Thurmond was born December 5, 1902 in Edgefield
County, South Carolina, to John Thurmond and Eleanor Strom. Always a studious young man, Thurmond enrolled at Clemson College (now Clemson University) at the age of 16. He was a member
of Phi Kappa Alpha fraternity; played a variety of sports including
football, baseball, basketball, and track; and graduated with a degree in horticulture. Immediately upon graduation, Thurmond
found work as a teacher in his hometown of Edgefield, South Carolina. He was fiercely committed at this early age to healthful living and applied this commitment by incorporating nutrition and
fitness into all of the curriculum he developed. In addition to teaching young people, he worked with local families to improve their
home gardens by planting healthier vegetables and fruits, as well
as fruit trees. He taught women about techniques for healthier
cooking. He nearly single-handedly developed athletic programs
in the local schools. (Cohodas 1993; Washington-Williams and
Stadiem 2005) His first political office was superintendent of education for Edgefield County, which he held during the early 1930s.
As with other individuals we have profiled in this book, Thurmond
was drawn to legal studies because he saw the law as a career that
would allow him to earn a better salary and support a family. Like
Jefferson, nearly 150 years before him, having attended law school
was not a requirement for entering the profession: instead, one
could study law independently and as soon as he (women were not
allowed to sit for the bar in South Carolina in the early 1930s),
could pass the bar, he was credentialed to practice. Thurmond studied with every free moment that he had and passed the bar in 1929
and began practicing law in Edgefield County.

Professional Life

Similarly, he had long been drawn to politics. Thurmond's father had been very active behind the scenes in politics, acting in the role we would now describe as campaign manager or campaign strategist. He managed the campaign of "Pitchfork" Ben Tillman. Tillman was one of the fiercest White supremacists and, as governor of South Carolina in the late 1800s, he was largely the architect of Jim Crow in South Carolina.[1] Though Thurmond's father was a significantly less virulent racist, Strom's exposure to Tillman's ideologies and rhetorical style on the "stump" greatly influenced his own political campaigns and his invocation of racist and segregationist ideology, especially during the height of the civil rights movement. (Cohodas 1993; Washington-Williams and Stadiem 2005) Indeed Thurmond made a promise to himself that he would one day be governor of South Carolina—a pact he made when at nine years old he watched Tillman debate and stump.

Thurmond had a long and varied career in public service that included serving in the South Carolina Senate, election to an Eleventh Circuit judgeship, serving as governor of the state of South Carolina and finally serving as the state's U.S. Senator, a post he held until his death in 2003.

During the early 1940s, moved by the atrocities of Hitler's regime, Thurmond left his judgeship to serve his country during World War II. He was a decorated war hero; he received eighteen medals for his service; including a Purple Heart and Bronze Star, in part

---

1. This is the same Tillman who disfranchised most African American men in South Carolina. The late Rayford W. Logan, in his book *The Negro in American Life and Thought: The Nadir, 1877–1901*, New York: Collier Books, quotes Tillman saying (p. 91):

> "We have done our level best to prevent blacks from voting. We have scratched our heads to find out how we could eliminate the last one of them. We stuffed ballot boxes. We shot them. We are not ashamed of it."

for his role in liberating Buchenwald. His most notable accomplishment was crash-landing his glider from the 82nd Airborne Division. Though many American men felt the call to fight in WWII, two issues made Thurmond's service unique: his age and the fact that he was a sitting judge. His daughter, Essie Mae Washington-Williams, provides her own insight. She suggests in her memoir (Washington-Williams and Stadiem 2005) that during the period from the mid-1920s until near the time of her mother's death in the late 1940s, that Thurmond and her mother carried on a long-term affair. Because her mother lived in Philadelphia, Washington-Williams suggests that Thurmond took advantage of the fact that being in the military would allow him to be stationed at bases in the Northeast, which would allow him to have more regular contact with Washington-Williams' mother, Carrie Butler. Given Thurmond's position as a federal judge, it seems highly likely that he could have had more power in dictating the terms of his military service than the average person, thus lending credence to Washington-Williams' claim.

Upon returning from World War II, Thurmond pursued his lifelong goal and in 1946 was elected as the governor of South Carolina. Thurmond ran as a Democrat and campaigned avidly as a segregationist. (Cohodas 1993; Washington-Williams and Stadiem 2005)

Thurmond, like many Southern politicians in the late 1940s, was appalled at what he saw happening to the national Democratic Party under the leadership of President Harry Truman. When Truman proposed various pieces of civil rights legislation, Southern Democrats viewed this as yet another "Yankee" attempt at reconstruction and they organized a "states rights" convention. Thurmond gave a fiery speech—a paragraph of which forms the epigram of this chapter—and was immediately tapped to run as a third party candidate—sponsored by the aptly named Dixiecrat party—against Truman. Thurmond lost, but admitted later that his hope was simply to draw enough Southern Democratic support away from Truman so that Republican Eisenhower could win the election. Thurmond carried four states: his home state of South Carolina, as well as the Deep South states of Alabama, Mississippi and Louisiana, where his message of segregation played loud and clear.[2]

Having lost his next bid for governor and having tasted national politics in his bid for the presidency, in 1954 Thurmond decided to run for the U.S. Senate. Because of his public support for the Republican President Eisenhower, Thurmond was blocked by the Democratic party, which refused to give him the nomination, forcing him to run as a write-in candidate. He is the only U.S. Senator *ever* to be elected as a write-in candidate. After continued tension between Thurmond and his party, he became a Republican in the 1960s. Thurmond reached the highest point in his career in 1981 when he became President pro tempore of the Senate, a post he held for three terms.

Thurmond openly supported Barry Goldwater, Richard Nixon, and John Connelly for president. Throughout most of his life, Thurmond supported segregation publicly. In addition to his run as a Dixiecrat, he is most well known for his filibuster speech on the Senate floor in 1957:

> Fortified with a good rest, a steam bath and a sirloin steak, Sen. Strom Thurmond talked against a 1957 civil rights bill for 24 hours and 18 minutes—longer than anyone has ever talked about anything in Congress. (Fox News 2003)

Thurmond modified his position on civil rights considerably across his career such that by the 1980s he supported the extension of the Voting Rights Act and the legislation making Martin Luther King Jr.'s birthday a national holiday. (Cohodas 1993; Washington-Williams and Stadiem 2005) Cohodas (1993: 11) summarizes it nicely:

---

2. It's interesting to note that during the 2008 presidential election, these four states once again distinguished themselves from the nation by voting en masse for the Republican nominee for President—John McCain—whereas the American population as a whole voted overwhelmingly for the Democratic nominee for president—Barack Obama.

On June 18, 1982, a typical warm day in Washington, D.C., Strom Thurmond, the senior Senator from South Carolina, officially left the Old South and arrived in the New. The trip that afternoon was only a quarter-mile, but the journey had taken thirty-four years. The senator had been to the floor of the United States Senate ten thousand times before to listen, to speak, and to vote, and as he made his way from his office in the stately Russell Building to the Capitol, nothing on the surface seemed out of the ordinary. But when he entered the Senate chamber shortly before two and answered the roll call on passage of the 1982 Voting Rights Act, Thurmond made his personal history. It was the first time in his long career that he had ever supported a civil rights bill, legislation that confirmed the federal government's role in protecting the freedom and opportunities bequeathed to all Americans by the United States Constitution.

Romantic Relationships/Family Life

Thurmond married his first wife, Jean Crouch, in 1947, when he was the governor of South Carolina. Thurmond was 44 and his wife, a homecoming queen, was 21. Despite their age difference, they quickly became not only the "first family" of South Carolina, but indeed the first family of the South. (Washington-Williams and Stadiem 2005) After Thurmond's election to the U.S. Senate in 1954, they moved to Washington where Thurmond reports Jean was well liked and that she and Senator John F. Kennedy's wife, Jacquelyn, were "friends and the beauties of the Senate." (Washington-Williams-Stadiem 2005: 178) Jean died tragically of a brain tumor in 1960—she was only 31 years old and they had not yet started a family. According to his daughter, Essie Mae Washington-Williams (Washington-Williams and Stadiem 2005), Thurmond was devastated and threw himself into his work.

Thurmond married his second wife, Nancy Moore, in 1968. He was 66 years old and much like her predecessor, Nancy was only

22 years old when they married! His daughter Essie Mae joked in her memoir that one of her father's few vices was his attraction to beautiful and *very young* women. (Washington-Williams and Stadiem 2005:189) Nancy had been awarded the title "Miss South Carolina" three years before they were wed and had nearly won the title "Miss America." Thurmond and Moore had four children together, the first when he was 68 years of age. His oldest daughter, Nancy Moore Thurmond, a beauty pageant contestant and a budding jewelry designer, was killed by a drunk driver in 1993. His son, James Thurmond Jr., is a member of the South Carolina Department of Natural Resources Law Enforcement Advisory Committee. His second daughter, Juliana Whitmer, is the spouse of a Washington, D.C. lawyer, and his son, Paul Thurmond, is a Charleston County council member. In 1991, Thurmond and Moore separated but never divorced. Thurmond's daughter Essie Mae Washington-Williams writes that the separation was difficult for her father and that South Carolinians were not generous in their assessment (Washington-Williams and Stadiem 2005:205):

> In 1991, Nancy Thurmond sought a separation from my father. Many South Carolinians, dubious of this May-December romance, believed that Nancy had married my father thinking he would soon pass away, and that she would "inherit" his Senate seat, as had another bright and ambitious southern belle, Lindy Boggs of Louisiana, when her powerful husband died in a plane crash. When my father lived on, and on, and on, the word was that she got depressed and simply couldn't take it anymore. "I suppose she wanted her freedom," he said to me in a rare moment of helplessness.

As Thurmond's health declined he lived first in a suite at Walter Reed Army Medical Center where he was escorted by nurses to the Senate each day for work, and finally, too debilitated to work, he passed his last days in a suite designed especially for him at the hospital in Edgefield County, South Carolina, where he passed away on June 26, 2003. He had served for nearly five decades in the U.S. Senate, where he was the oldest member.

Interracial Relationships/Couplings

Just months after Thurmond's death, one of his daughters, Essie Mae Washington-Williams (Staples 2003), whose mother was an African American maid in his parents' home, came forward to establish her birthright.

According to newspaper accounts (Staples 2003), Strom Thurmond had sexual relations with Carrie Butler. He was 22 and living in his parents' house and she was 15 and working as a maid—she was 16 when their daughter, Essie Mae Washington, was born. Had we relied exclusively on the journalistic accounts of these events, which we did at first, we might have come to the conclusion that the liaison that resulted in Essie Mae Washington's birth was a one-night stand at best and non-consensual at worst. indeed, this is the history of relations between White men and Black women in the South. (Omi and Winant 1986) Yet, as the majority of "cases" presented in this book document, these relationships are typically far more complex than meets the eye. And, based on the first-hand account provided by Essie Mae Washington-Williams in her memoir, we can move beyond the journalistic accounts to examine not only the complex relationship between Thurmond and Carrie Butler, but also the complexities this relationship created for Thurmond himself.

According to various accounts—though curiously its mention is completely absent in Cohodas' biography—Strom Thurmond's paternity, the knowledge of the "relationship" between Mr. Thurmond and Carrie Butler and the child that resulted from this union were well known in the small community of Edgefield, South Carolina. In recounting conversations with her Aunt Calliope, Essie Mae Washington-Williams reports that she learned a great deal about the norms and regulations around inter-racial sexuality in the "Old South ... and in the New" and the way in which her own particular story fit into this context. (Washington-Williams and Stadiem 2005: 53)

> Aunt Calliope explained the bizarre double standard of interracial sexuality in the Old South, which continued in the New.... Any sexual relationship between

a White woman and a Black man was immediately presumed to be rape of the most brutal kind. But White men, on the other hand, were entitled, by nearly divine right, to have the run of the henhouse, or slave quarters. 'The massas all looked after their children, no matter who birthed them. That was part of what it meant to be a gentleman,'. . . Calliope knew about my father, my real White father — everybody in my family did. Only I had been in the dark. (Washington-Williams and Stadiem 2005: 53–54)

From the outside, because Thurmond did not discuss his relationship with Carrie Butler nor did he publicly acknowledge his parentage of Essie Mae, it might appear that Thurmond was denying these relationships, and we certainly believed this when we first read the accounts of Essie Mae Washington-Williams published in the *New York Times* at the time of Thurmond's death. But, accounts provided by Washington-Williams and her relatives suggest a different story.

After the Civil War, despite the kings having been deposed, the kingly style continued ... Each young man took a former slave as a common-law wife and had children with her. These mixed-race offspring all grew up in the great house, accepted as part of one happy family. 'Pickens and pickaninnies.'. . . what Strom Thurmond was doing with me, then, was part of a long Edgefield tradition. Another aunt told me that Judge Thurmond was supporting my mother; that was why she didn't have to work. (Washington-Williams and Stadiem 2005: 54–55)

In the tradition of the Southern gentleman that Aunt Calliope described, though Thurmond did not meet his daughter, Essie Mae, for the first time until she was 17 years old, and he often allowed years to pass without contacting her — the longest being the time he was in Europe fighting in World War II — Thurmond did in fact have a relationship with Essie Mae. In her book, she recounts his visits. After meeting her for the first time in Edgefield, South Carolina, during a visit Essie Mae made with Carrie and her aunt, Carrie's sister, who at the time Essie Mae believed to be her own mother, Thurmond visited Essie Mae during trips he made through the northern cities in which she lived, including Philadelphia and New York. And, though Essie Mae writes that she wished for the more loving and affectionate relationship that she had with the men Mary, her aunt who raised her, married, she acknowledges that Thurmond not only supported her financially, but during their meetings he offered her advice on his favorite topics, including health/fitness and especially education.

During a visit Thurmond made to New York in the spring of 1946, as Essie Mae was in her first year in nursing school and had come to the conclusion that she wanted instead to pursue a career in education, he counseled her about attending a four-year college. Initially he threw out suggestions such as Harvard and Wellesley, which stunned Essie Mae. Then, realizing how expensive the tuition at these schools would be, he suggested she think about attending a school in South Carolina.

> I decided I had no better option than to accept my father's "scholarship" to attend Orangeburg, whose official name, according to its small and modest catalog, was The Colored Normal, Industrial, Agricultural, and Mechanical College of South Carolina. Nothing on the educational earth could have seemed farther from Harvard. That my father could speak of them in the same breath was a comment on either his intense South Carolina chauvinism or an equally intense racial myopia. As long as Black students weren't darkening the door of his beloved Clemson or the majestic University of South Carolina, any school they went to was just "fine" with him. (Washington-Williams and Stadiem 2005: 100)

This is one of the clearest examples Essie Mae provides of her complex relationship with her father. Though he wanted the best for her and believed she was worthy of it—he had first suggested she think about applying to Harvard and Wellesley—he was not able to move past his cultural and ideological beliefs that were so deeply and firmly rooted in the racial ideology of segregation. He was unwilling to fight to have Essie Mae admitted to his alma mater, Clemson University, nor to the flag ship university in the state — the University of South Carolina — so instead he not only advocated for her to enroll in South Carolina State, but as Governor he invested a great deal of the state's money in improving that institution; his goal was to create *equal accommodations* for Blacks with the intent that they remain *separate*.

One of the most difficult aspects of the relationship between Thurmond and his daughter Essie Mae — in addition to the fact that it was secret — was that for many years Thurmond did not verbally describe his relationship to Essie Mae as "father and daughter." Essie Mae recounts the first time that Thurmond did. It was in 1947 and he had recently been elected governor. On this particular visit, Thurmond began with what would become his favorite question: "How does it feel to be the daughter of the governor?" (Washington-Williams and Stadiem 2005:124) This was also the first time that Thurmond hugged — rather than shook hands — with Essie Mae when they parted. She recalls that this was incredibly significant for her.

Thurmond made regular, often monthly visits to South Carolina State — as Orangeburg was called — to visit Essie Mae. His visits were "officially" to discuss higher education with the president of South Carolina State, though Essie Mae assumes that the president understood the truth of these visits. It's hard to imagine the state governor coming to a "Black college" so regularly and always visiting with the same student! And, indeed by her second year at State, rumors began circulating on campus that Governor Thurmond was visiting a young woman who was his daughter. One of the fairest girls on campus was the target of the rumors, and though Essie Mae recalled that should would have liked to have rescued her fellow classmate from the rumor mill, she had to remain quiet about her ancestry. (Washington-Williams and Stadiem 2005: 130)

Essie Mae recounts in her memoir the details of a lengthy — nearly 65 years — relationship with her father, but also provides insight into his relationship with her mother. Essie Mae and her father talked on the phone regularly, she visited him in his Senate chambers and in his final years at his home in Edgefield, South Carolina. The context for these visits, which were often very public, was that Essie Mae — and her children, who later accompanied her on these visits — were "old family friends" from South Carolina. Though Essie Mae clearly desired her father's public acknowledgement of their relationship — which she received after his death, when her name was added to the list of his children on the monument to him outside the state house in Columbia, South Carolina — she agreed that his description was nevertheless appropriate: they were both "family" and "friends."

Essie Mae also provides insight into the relationship between Thurmond and her mother, Carrie Butler. Though as a young woman Essie Mae was reluctant to discuss the intimate details of their relationship — as any daughter would likely be — she provides ample evidence to conclude that Thurmond and Butler carried on a multiple decade relationship that began in the early 1920s and ended just prior to Butler's death in 1947. Essie Mae recounts many conversations she had with her mother that included enough details to confirm that her mother and Thurmond spoke regularly; as noted earlier, there is evidence that he spent a great deal of time with Butler during his stint in the military during WWII — a period when her mother spent little time with Washington-Williams herself. And, perhaps the most poignant evidence comes from the conversation Essie Mae had with Thurmond in which she confronted him about his then recent marriage (Washington-Williams and Stadiem 2005:144):

> "You got married, Governor," I boldly said, unafraid, for once, of being imprudent. "Not before she ..." He let his voice trail off. He was implying that my mother had taken up with George (a man with whom she lived) before he took up with Jean. I had no idea who came first ...

And told him of her mother's recent death (Washington-Williams and Stadiem 2005:144):

> ... I blurted out, "My mother is dead." ... He leaned in to me and, in a near-whisper, said "I truly cared for that woman. She was a wonderful person. A won-

derful woman … I can't.…" Then his voice trailed
off into silence.

Finally, Essie Mae Washington-Williams makes it abundantly clear
in her memoir that her relationship with her father was complex and
that her feelings for him were complex as well.

For example, she was mortified when she watched him deliver
speeches in which he called for the maintenance of a system of segregation in the South; a system that so clearly oppressed her, his
daughter. But, to her credit, as their relationship grew and weath-
ered the changing social-political-economic landscape, Essie Mae
confronted her father on matters of race and she made it her mis-
sion to spend as much time as she could with him hoping that his
increased exposure to what her life — as a Black woman — was like
would modify his racial ideology and beliefs about segregation.

Finally, though many people have been publicly very critical of
Essie Mae Washington-Williams for this, she expresses, throughout
the memoir, her gratitude for all of the financial support that Thurmond provided her across her life and all of the other types of support, including a naval commission for her son and powerful
appointments for her college friends, that he provided. Though
some, including her husband and Staples (2003), charge that Thurmond's support was "hush money," Essie Mae's assessment is kinder.
Early on, her family members disclosed the fact that Thurmond
provided for her and her mother financially. We offer that a gen-
tler interpretation of this is that these payments were not all that different from modern day spousal and child support. Aren't we critical
of men — especially those with power and privilege — who *don't*
provide this? Secondly, as we will argue in the conclusion, these
payments and Thurmond's support can be interpreted as consistent
with his ideology of segregation: *separate but equal.*

Conclusion

Even though on the surface he had it all, high office, a
perfect wife, health and wealth and power, I — and only

I—knew how deeply conflicted he had to be. (Washington-Williams and Stadiem 2005: 148)

The Civil War ended just thirty-seven years before Thurmond was born and his connection to his grandfather's experiences as a Confederate soldier—who recounted the story of his walking back to South Caroline from Appomattox after losing his horse in battle—was "as real to young Strom as if it had happened to him." (Cohodas 1993: 12) Clearly the impact of these experiences—typical of young White Southern men at the turn of the 20th Century—profoundly impacted Thurmond's racial ideology and his political career. As Cohodas (1993: 12–13) writes:

> Senator Strom Thurmond shared the fierce pride most white southerners felt about "the War Between the States," as they called it, and in every civil rights bill he saw deliberate punishment of his homeland. He fought each one, and threw his rhetorical might against every Supreme Court decision protecting minorities from discrimination.

Like many White Southerners of his generation, he saw the federal government's actions as tools for punishing the South—a virtual continuation of the Civil War—and he saw non-Southerners who engaged in freedom rides and marches as "outside agitators." (Cohodas 1993:13) But, as Cohodas (1993: 13) argues, the civil rights movement, which was largely centered in Thurmond's home state of South Carolina, and the actors in the movement " ... made the senator an involuntary participant in the civil rights movement."

Though the turbulence of the Civil Rights movement challenged many White Southerners, among them Thurmond's peers who served as U.S. Senators, Representatives and Governors, according to Cohodas (1993), Thurmond was not only far more rigid in his racial ideology but also more actively resisted any movement by the federal government to require integration than his Southern political peers.

While other senators voted with what they perceived to be the prevailing White interests, Thurmond stoked the fires of resistance in countless speeches, press releases, and reports to his constituents, and this is what set him apart. He was a cheerleader for segregation, even if the cheers he led were not always couched in racial terms but in the antiseptic rhetoric of states' rights. (Cohodas 1993: 14)

Yet, as fiercely as Thurmond opposed integration, he was equally opposed to unfair treatment of "Negroes" (clearly he didn't define segregation as "unfair") and violence. For example, though other Southern Democrats publicly defended lynching as a tool for protecting White women from "Negro" men, Thurmond never invoked this particular racist ideology and in fact abhorred it. Thurmond's daughter, Essie Mae Washington-Williams recalls that the first "test" to his ideology was the 1947 lynching of an African American man in Greenville, South Carolina. To her surprise, not only did Thurmond stand up against the lynching, he collaborated with the FBI and northern groups who came to seek justice — even if unsuccessfully — in the trial of the men who committed the lynching. (Washington-Williams and Stadiem 2005: 122)

Scholars and biographers disagree about the degree to which Strom Thurmond's racism was completely embedded in the fiber of his being. Cohodas (1993) is clear that Thurmond continued to express his racist ideology until the early 1980s when, she argues, he could no longer ignore the African American vote. His daughter, Essie Mae Washington-Williams, agrees that he held on to his racist politics well into the last decades of the 20th century, but comparing his response to the 1947 lynching in contrast to the ideology he expressed in his public speeches at the Democratic governors' conference in late 1948, she argues that Thurmond became more viciously racist in his public speeches as a direct response to his marriage to his first wife, Jean Crouch, whom he had married earlier that year. (Washington-Williams and Stadiem 2005) Crouch was a 21-year-old homecoming queen and Thurmond a 46-year-old governor when they married and Washington-Williams argues that

his staunch defending of the Southern way of life was highly influenced by his new "duty" to protect all Southern White women in
South Carolina from the uncivilized African American man. (Washington-Williams and Stadiem 2005: 133–134)

Similarly, journalists argue that Thurmond was worried about
the impact on his political life should his relationship with Carrie Butler and the fathering of a "Black" daughter become public and they
charge that Thurmond's financial support of his daughter was in
fact "hush money." (Staples 2003) Certainly, as this book demonstrates, Thurmond's relationship with Carrie Butler and his fathering of their daughter—Essie Mae Washington-William—was not
all that unusual for a Southern man of means, as noted by Essie
Mae's Aunt Calliope. Yet, some have noted that once it became clear
that Mr. Thurmond had set his sights on a political career that would
take him *out of the South*, it became critical that this relationship
and this child remain a secret. (Staples 2003) Why? Because outside
of the South this was never commonplace. And, the various newspaper headlines that "suggested" that the fierce segregationist had a
"Black" daughter certainly provide support for this proposition.

Furthermore, Essie Mae's own revelations in her memoir reveal
that both she and Thurmond understood the potential consequences
of this truth. She notes, for example, that when she lived in California and he wired her money that the return address was undis-
closed or that when she mailed him Father's Day cards, she received
notes in return that were written by staffers—just as any constituent
would. That said, Essie Mae makes it clear throughout her memoir that Thurmond never swore her to secrecy or even asked her to
keep their relationship secret, though she did until he died. "Strom
Thurmond never swore me to secrecy. He never swore me to anything. He trusted me, and I respected him, and we loved each other
in our deeply repressed ways, and that was our social contract."
(Washington-Williams and Stadiem 2005: 190) Thus, the suggestion that Thurmond's financial support of his daughter was "hush
money" is perhaps unfounded.

The goal in this book has been to try to understand the complex lives of men who expressed public views about race that seem

contradictory to their lived realities. The case of Strom Thurmond not only presents this same dilemma but is perhaps the most difficult to disentangle. We conclude this chapter by offering a lens with which to understand Thurmond's life.

Perhaps the most shocking part of the Thurmond debacle is that Thurmond was such a staunch segregationist. Thurmond, who had a "Black" daughter, severely opposed school integration and ran on the segregationist ticket in the 1948 Presidential election. His platform revolved around maintaining the sanctity of the Southern way of life: maintaining and enforcing racial boundaries through a complex system of segregation. Any equitable treatment of Thurmond's political career, however, cannot end with his 1948 run for the presidency. As the longest serving senator in U.S. history and a man whose life spanned the entire 20th Century, his longevity offers an opportunity for change. What was the source of that change?

We quoted, at length, Cohodas' (1993) analysis that though it took many years for Thurmond to modify his position on race and segregation, he eventually did, in response to the increased voting power of Black men and women in South Carolina. His daughter, citing similar examples, including the fact that nearly a decade before his vote on the Voting Rights Act in 1982, he became the first Southern senator ever to recommend a Black man for a federal judgeship,Matthew Perry, who was appointed by Thurmond to the U.S. Court of Military Appeals—in 1974—suggests an alternative explanation. Matthew Perry was Essie Mae's first boyfriend. When sharing with her the news about his appointment, Thurmond made it clear that the reason he chose Perry was not only that he was an excellent lawyer—he had distinguished himself as one of the top lawyers in the South, even serving as chief counsel for the NAACP—but because if he had dated Essie Mae, he must be a good man. Thus, Essie Mae Washington-Williams believes that Thurmond's moderation of his racial ideology over his lifetime was in part a result of his continuous relationship with her, which provided him clear evidence that despite his desire to believe that separate could be equal, this belief was fundamentally flawed.

To many studying his life, Thurmond's seems a series of contradictions. Essie Mae Washington-Williams herself asked: "How could the son of this architect of White supremacy fall in love with my mother, a Black women? ... Carrie (her mother) shrugged, rather enigmatically. 'Love is love. It's color blind. Besides,' she added, 'all that hate talk is just politics.'" (Washington-Williams and Stadiem 2005: 41) And, were it just his life, perhaps we could understand it as a personality deficiency. However, when we add Thurmond and Jefferson and so many others to this story, we begin to see that the contradictions were not in the person, but rather in the cultural traditions and institutions of the South.

In the years since Thurmond's death, Essie Mae Washington-Williams has been very public about her ancestry: she did a nationally televised interview with Dan Rather, was written about by *New York Times* reporter Brent Staples, and made a public claim as an inheritor to Thurmond's estate. One necessarily wonders how this news of Essie Mae Washington as the first daughter of Strom Thurmond has been received by the "White" Thurmonds? A *New York Times* article (Staples 2003) reports that they are concerned about the way this news paints them in the community. Yet, according to Essie Mae Washington-Williams' memoir, she has established "friendly" relationships with Thurmond's widow Nancy, his son Strom Jr., and other family members. (Washington-Williams and Stadiem 2005: 220) Perhaps the time between Staples' article and Washington-Williams memoir has softened the "White" Thurmonds, or perhaps Staples and Washington-Williams differ in their evaluation of the reaction of the "White" Thurmonds. In any case, as Staples (2003) points out, Thurmond and Washington-Williams' incredibly complex life is a microcosm of race relations and family histories across the United States, and especially across the South. The complexities of their lives force us to examine the incredible complexities of race and the social history of the United States.

There is ample evidence that Thurmond's particular racial ideology defined Blacks as "different but not inferior." (Washington-Williams and Stadiem 2005: 146) Segregation, then, was not in violation of Thurmond's racial ideology, but differential treatment was. It is revealing that when his daughter, Essie Mae, pushed him on his claims made at the states' rights convention that "Negroes" should not be allowed to swim in "our" swimming pools, he responded, shocked by her accusation, that as governor he had provided the funds to build swimming pools in "Negro" communities. Similarly, he argued that education was the key to raising "Negroes" out of poverty and to that end he reminded Essie Mae that he invested tremendous resources in South Carolina State for that very reason. Thurmond saw himself as a Roosevelt progressive, who advocated for the improvement of the lives of "Negroes" and the poor through a variety of social programs and the funding of education. But, in contrast to Roosevelt, this brand of progressive politics was shaped by Thurmond's strongly held belief that Blacks and Whites must pursue the American Dream in a separate—but he hoped equal—landscape. This insight helps us to better capture what appears to be such a contradiction in the life of Strom Thurmond.

In concluding this discussion, we suggest that, just as Jefferson developed an ideology of racial inferiority in order to deal with the contractions in his life and the dissonance it must have created, Thurmond, living a century later, developed an ideology of "separate but equal" that allowed him to reduce the dissonance in his own life. A "separate but equal" ideology allowed him to love a "Black" woman, even though he knew they could never live together. A "separate but equal" ideology allowed him to advocate for and finance his "Black" daughter's education without challenging exclusionary doctrines at prestigious Southern universities nor without believing that he was subjecting his daughter to an inferior—if segregated—education.

This interpretation of Thurmond's ideologies helps to shed light on what appear to be contradictions in his behaviors. That said, as with Jefferson, we suggest that unfortunately Thurmond did not have the power to ensure "separate but equal" beyond his personal life. Where he was perhaps able to provide his daughter with the "best money can buy," his insistence on seeking individual solutions to his dilemma rather than focusing on systemic change meant that millions of African Americans lived for decades under Jim Crow segregation, being forced to endure *unequal and often inhumane* conditions, while Thurmond fiercely led the battle to maintain segregation. Had Thurmond instead sought institutional rather than individual solutions to his dilemma, we can only imagine that integration may have come sooner and more swiftly to his "kingdom" of South Carolina.

Chapter Ten

Conclusion: What Lessons Can We Draw?

The obsession in the United States about interracial relationships is both overwhelming and intriguing; overwhelming because of its volume and intriguing because of the incredibly low numbers of individuals who actually choose to involve themselves in interracial couplings. In fact, only 4 percent of Whites marry outside of their race. Yet, because Whites make up nearly 70 percent of the U.S. population, 92 percent of interracial marriages involve a White partner. In contrast, 9 percent of African Americans and 60 percent of Asians marry outside of their race, with the majority of these marriages involving a White partner. The most common configuration of interracial marriage involves a White man and an Asian woman (40 percent of Asian women are married to White men) and the least common involve White men and African American women (1.5 percent of White men marry African American women). Thus, we can conclude that Whites and Blacks are the least likely to marry outside their race, regardless of who their partners are, whereas Asians are *more likely to marry outside their race than they are to marry a same-race partner.* (See Figure 10-1.)

Interracial intimate relationships are a curious thing. They are few and far between, yet they stir a lot of interest. For example, the combination of a White male and an Asian female, by far the majority of interracial couplings in the United States, has few onlookers. The coupling of an African American male and a White female, a rare coupling among all race-ethnic couplings, attracts a lot of attention.

For a variety of complex reasons, in the United States, most Americans marry within their own race/ethnic and religious

Figure 10-1: Percentage of Married and Cohabiting Americans in Interracial Relationships

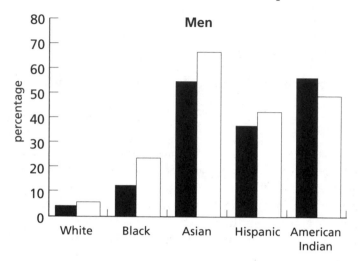

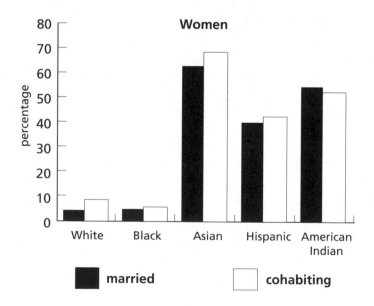

(Qian 2005)

groups—approximately 90 percent of all marriages are intraracial. Family sociologists call this *homogamy.* (Qian and Lichter 2007)

While strict sanctions against out-group relationships and marriage have declined, there is still a strong cultural taboo against it.[1] As university faculty who year in and year out teach courses on the family and social stratification, we routinely hear accounts from students from a variety of race/ethnic groups who confess their parents' disdain when they chose to cross the "color-line" when dating.

This book is thus focused on a topic of incredible intrigue for people living in the United States. Yet, unlike the majority of researchers who examine interracial couplings by analyzing trends exhibited in census data, we explored interracial relationships by situating them in the context of stratification: a system in which some people have power over others and a very small number of people have the power to influence the way others think.

The complexities of interracial relationships are very deep. When we look at the demographics of where Blacks lived up until recently, we see that they resided mostly in the South. It is in the South that we see the strictest norms forbidding the crossing of racial lines to establish intimate relationships. The archives of injustices are full of examples of public lynchings, castrations, and torturous murder that are detailed in many research articles and books on the South. Not un-coincidentally the last states to hold on to statutes prohibiting interracial marriages were in the South.

Given the strong prohibitions against interracial marriages in the South, it is curious to those examining these relationships for the first time to note that the South is also the geographic location where the rate of interracial couplings is the highest.

As sociologists who study the family, we can interpret this seeming contradiction by looking to the vast sociological research that

---

1. It is only since 1967 that all sanctions against interracial relationships have been legally ended. Of course, the lag-time is great for cultural acceptance of these relationships. See especially Hattery and Smith (ed.) 2009 *Interracial Relationships.*

demonstrates the fact that most people meet their future partners, wives, husbands in the places where they have the most intimate interactions (e.g., neighborhoods, churches, work, school, etc.) — sociologists refer to this process as "propinquity" — and thus it is not surprising that the close relationships historically between Whites and Blacks, especially in the South, should produce intimate relationships across racial boundaries.

In fact, the taboos against these relationships grew out of this closeness and in direct response to the fact that these relationships — though almost exclusively between White men and African American women — had been taking place ever since the beginning of slavery. The group of people known to us as mulattos are the result of these intimate relationships. (Johnson 1970, p. 217) They serve as proof of the intimacies across the "color line." Johnson put it thus:

> Vice to a most shameful extent is proved by the rapid increase of mulattoes.

What is very complex in terms of understanding these interracial intimate relationships in the "Old South" was the social structure of the South. Historian Wyatt-Brown in his award-winning book entitled *Southern Honor: Ethics and Behavior in the Old South* concludes that it was a defense of male integrity that was fundamental to Southern culture. In this patriarchal social formation, White men were in full control, and all females (White and Black) endured their lot silently. (Wyatt-Brown 1982, p. 34)

Does this excuse the exploitation in these power relationships? No. Yet, our analysis of these relationships shows them for what they were; many couples, many people, live with contradictions in their lives. Some interracial couples, for example, address the race/ethnic issues coming at them by dealing with them directly — negotiating race — while others ignore issues of race, stratification and power. Both of these responses can be best understood as strategies that individuals and couples employ to deal with what the culture still deems contested terrain.

For example, as we detailed in the previous chapter, the case of Senator Strom Thurmond demonstrates the complex manner in which he navigated his relationship to his lover and his daughter. As we uncovered Thurmond, we found he was far more complex than his Dixiecrat label suggests.

First off, he loved Carrie Butler. He loved his mulatto daughter, Essie Mae. We can argue that both time and circumstances did not allow him to publicly show this; furthermore had he chosen to bring his relationship into public view he would have paid a heavy price. As the writer Malcolm Gladwell shows in *Outliers*, social ostracism would be the price to pay for publicly displaying intimacy with someone of another race, especially during the time of miscegenation. (177)

Unlike Thurmond—or Jefferson or Thomas, or the others whose lives are detailed in this book—most people are not in a position to shape policy or ideology. This is what makes this book different from all others that address this issue.

Clarence Thomas, the Supreme Court Justice, for example, can take his privilege of position on the "high court" and impact the lives of thousands if not millions of people. Turning back the progress in Civil Rights legislation while simultaneously holding down the seat of the "dean" of Civil Rights, the late U.S. Supreme Court Justice Thurgood Marshall, is a case in point. The same goes for President Thomas Jefferson and Senator Strom Thurmond, although Thurmond might, in the end, be the "outlier."

The impetus for this book came from a project we were working on that explores the "cultural contradictions" of the South. As non-Southerners we were perplexed by the fact that Southern culture and norms of behavior allowed for some of the most intimate kinds of cross-racial interactions—such as the employment of African American women as wet-nurses for White children—while simultaneously prohibiting—through the series of complex Jim Crow laws—behaviors like drinking from the same water fountain that seemed to us decidedly less intimate than interactions such as wet-nursing.

Clearly, the most intimate relationship one can have is with a sexual partner. Thus, we were immediately drawn to figures such as Thomas Jefferson, who we knew owned slaves while simultaneously having a long-term sexual relationship with Sally Hemings, his own slave. We pondered, how can a man own the woman he loves?

In fairness to Jefferson, we do have to acknowledge the fact that until very recently, women have been considered the property of men—first their fathers and later their husbands (Hattery 2008)—but even that fact did not allow husbands to sell their wives. Thus, there is a vast distinction between "women as the property of their husbands" and chattel slaves.

Thus, our initial question regarding Jefferson propelled us toward asking more questions. What is equally intriguing about Jefferson is the fact that his position as a Founding Father and early president of the United States provided him the opportunity to enter his beliefs into public discourse through his writing. Jefferson was a prolific writer, but perhaps most interesting is the fact that he is most famous for penning the Declaration of Independence—the modern day tome on equality and human rights. Thus, our interest expanded beyond what seemed to be inherent contradictions in people's lives to an examination of these contradictions in the lives of individuals who had a publicly accessible discourse on human rights, inequality, race and/or race relations.

As we began to scour historical figures—often at the urging of our historian colleagues—we also thought about contemporary figures that fit the requirements of our inquiry. What began as a project focused on Thomas Jefferson and Strom Thurmond soon expanded to a project that ranged from historic figures like George Washington to relatively unknown people such as Richard Mentor Johnson, to contemporary figures including Clarence Thomas and William Cohen.

Admittedly, when we first began writing the chapters in this book, we focused more on the individual contradictions that individual people lived with. As our research deepened, we began to realize that not only were the public writings of these individuals often in contrast to their lived realities, but because of their positions of prominence and power, their writings and ideologies not only entered the public discourse but shaped Americans' attitudes about equality, race, and interracial unions.

Thus, for figures such as Thomas Jefferson, Strom Thurmond, and Clarence Thomas, their writings and speeches—though perhaps created primarily to provide justification for their own circumstances and reduce their own cognitive dissonance—were consumed by policy makers and regular citizens. Thus, their *personal* ideologies shaped public policy with regards to race, interracial unions, and so forth.

As we noted in the respective chapters that explore Jefferson, Thurmond, and Thomas, the racial ideologies these men constructed in part to deal with their own lives, have shaped in very powerful ways the American racial discourse and policy. We argue that Jefferson's greatest legacy was not the Declaration of Independence, but rather his development of a racial ideology that constructed people of African descent as inferior. This, coupled with his unwillingness to oppose slavery—out of fear that the Union would collapse—contributed to the persistence of slavery for another 40 years, as well as contributed significantly to the hegemonic ideology on racial superiority that dominated the American landscape for 200 years and continues to be invoked by some today. At the individual level, his unwillingness to be honest about his relationship with Sally Hemings prevented him from emancipating her or their children which, according to Gordon-Reed (2008), contributed significantly to the destruction of Sally Hemings' and Jefferson's family.

Similarly, Strom Thurmond's attempts to deal with his own love relationship with Carrie Butler led to his development of a fervent ideology of racial segregation. He not only clung to but perpetuated the belief that the races ought to remain separate and that segregation was the tool to accomplish this. Despite every indication that separate can never be equal, Thurmond fought for decades for policies that would improve the lives of "Negroes" by investing in "their" institutions. Thurmond's position as a U.S. Senator meant that his perspective and influence were widely felt, and it is reasonable to assume that the delay of the relaxing of Jim Crow segregation, particularly in the Deep South, can in part be attributed to Thurmond. Thus, like Jefferson, Thurmond's attempts to resolve cognitive dissonance in his personal life had very public and widespread outcomes.

We close the book by suggesting that in cases such as Jefferson and Thurmond, and perhaps to a lesser degree Clarence Thomas, and in very different ways with regards to William Cohen, individual attempts to reconcile competing beliefs can impact both the dominant ideology but also public policy. This raises questions that are much larger than simply individuals' attitudes and policies regarding interracial relationships. We argue that the analysis in this chapter requires that scholars and citizens challenge the discourses of public figures, especially with regards to issues of equality. For example, as the newly elected president of the United States, Barack Obama, was putting togther his cabinet, there was much speculation about the suitability of Larry Summers, former president of Harvard University, for a high-level position in the U.S. Department of the Treasury based on some public statements Summers made asserting possible biologically based gender differences in aptitude for science and math.[2] Some have questioned whether his statements excluded him from serious consideration for the position of Secretary of Treasury in the Obama administration (he did accept a high level appointment on the President's economic advisory council). Others suggest that his comments were taken out of context, misunderstood, and exaggerated, and that he was the victim of a witch hunt by disgruntled Harvard faculty.

Whether Summers holds misogynistic beliefs is not for us to judge in the confines of this book, but our analysis here suggests that unless scholars and citizens properly interrogate creators of public discourse, hegemonic ideology, and public policy, we remain vulnerable to a future adversely shaped by individual beliefs and the ideologies powerful individuals construct to counter their own cognitive dissonance.

---

2. We point the interested reader to the MIT gender equality study: http://web.mit.edu/fnl/women/women.html.

Bibliography

2003. "Julia Chinn: Slave Mistress." *Southern History Net* http://www.southernhistory.net/modules.php?op=modload &name=News&file=article&sid=8704&mode=thread&order=0& thold=0

Aka, Philip. 2006. "The Supreme Court and Affirmative Action in Public Education, with Special Reference to the Michigan Cases." *Brigham Young University Education and Law Journal* 1: 11–95.

Aptheker, Herbert. 1951–1994. *A Documentary History of the Negro People in the United States*. 7 volumes. New York: Citadel Press.

Berry, Mary Francis. 1994. "Judging Morality: Sexual Behavior and Legal Consequences in the late Nineteenth Century South." Pp. 13–34 in Donald G. Nieman (ed.), *Black Southerners and the Law, 1865–1900*. New York: Taylor & Francis

Blassingame, John. 1979. *The Slave Community*. New York: Oxford University Press.

Bonilla-Silva, Eduardo. 2004. "The Many Costs of Racism." *Social Forces* 82: 1240–1242.

Bonilla-Silva, Eduardo. 2001. *White Supremacy and Racism in the Post Civil-Rights Era*. Boulder, CO: Lynn Rienner.

Bonilla-Silva, Eduardo. 2003. *Racism Without Racists: Color Blind Racism and the Persistence of Racial Inequality in the United States*. Latham, MD: Rowman & Littlefield.

Bryant, Linda Allen. 2004. I Cannot Tell A Lie: The True Story of George Washington's African American Descendants. Bloomington, IN: Universe Star.

Cohen, Janet Langhart. 2004. *From Rage To Reason: My Life in Two Americas*. New York: Kensington.

Cohen, William S. (with Janet Langhart Cohen). 2007. *Love in Black and White: A Memoir of Race, Religion and Romance.* Lantham, MD: Rowman and Littlefield.

Cohodas, Nadine. 1993. *Strom Thurmond.* New York: Simon and Schuster.

Correa, Michael Jones. 2001. "The Origins and Diffusion of Racial Restrictive Covenants." *Political Science Quarterly* 115: 541–568.

Davis, Angela. 1983. *Women, Race and Class.* New York: Vintage Books.

Davis, David Brion. 2006. *Inhuman Bondage: The Rise and Fall of Slavery in the New World.* New York: Oxford University Press.

Douglas, Davidson M. 1995. *Reading, Writing, & Race: The Desegregation of the Charlotte Schools.* Chapel Hill: North Carolina: University of North Carolina Press.

Douglass, Frederick. 1845. *Narratives of the Life of Frederick Douglass, An American Slave.* Boston, MA: The Anti-Slavery http://sunsite.berkeley.edu/Literature/Douglass/Autobiography/A1.html.

Douglass, Frederick. Nd. "Frederick Douglass Papers." Washington, DC: Library of Congress http://lcweb2.loc.gov/ammen/doughtml/dougFolder2.html.

Economist, The. Mildred Loving. May 15, 2008. Accessed online http://www.economist.com/obituary/displaystory.cfm?story_id=11 367685. November 12, 2008.

Epstein, Cynthia Fuchs. 2007. "Great Divides: The Cultural, Cognitive, and Social Bases of the Global subordination of Women." *American Sociological Review* 72:1–22.

Faragher, John. 1994. *Rereading Frederick Jackson Turner: The Significance of the Frontier in American History, and Other Essays.* New York: Henry Holt Company

Feagin, Joe R. 1991. "The Continuing Significance of Race: Antiblack Discrimination in Public Places." *American Sociological Review* 56:101–116.

Fehn, Bruce. 2000. Thomas Jefferson and Slaves: Teaching an American Paradox. *AH Magazine of History* 14(2). Accessed online:

Organization of American Historians: http://www.oah. org/images/namcplate0602.jpg. Accessed: November 8, 2008.

Ford, West. Nd. "The Biography of West Ford." The Legacy of West Ford. http://www.westfordlegacy.com/home.htm.

Fox News. 2003. Thurmond Holds Senate Record for Filibustering. June 27, 2003. Accessed on line: http://www.foxnews.com/story/0,2933,90552,00.html. November 12, 2008.

Foner, Eric. 2002. *Reconstruction: America's Unfinished Revolution, 1863–1877*. New York: Harper & Row.

Franz, Kathleen. 2001. "The Open Road: Automobility and Racial Uplift in the Inter-War Years." Center for the History of Business, Technology and Society, Wilmington, Delaware.

Gladwell, Malcolm. 2008. *Outliers: The Story of Success*. Boston: Little, Brown & Company.

Gordon-Reed, Annette. 2008. *The Hemingses of Monticello*. New York: W.W. Norton.

Grant, Colin. 2008. *Black Star: Negro With A Hat*. New York: Oxford University Press.

Greenhouse, Linda. 2008. "Justices Say Law Bars Retaliation Over Bias Claims" in *New York Times*. New York City.

Grutter v. Bollinger, 539 U.S. 982, 156 L. Ed. 2d 694, 124 S. Ct. 35, 2003 U.S. LEXIS 5357 (U.S., 2003)

Hattery, Angela J. 2008. *Intimate Partner Violence*. Latham, MD: Rowman & Littlefield.

Hattery, Angela and Earl Smith. 2007a. *African American Families*. Thousand Oaks, California: SAGE.

―――. 2007b. "Dred Scott, White Supremacy and African American Civil Rights." Pp. 445–47 in *International Encyclopedia of the Social Sciences*, edited by W. A. Darity. Farmington Hill, MI: Thomson Gale, Inc.

Hattery, Angela J. and Earl Smith. 2006. "Social Stratification in the New/Old South:The Influences of Racial Segregation on Social Class in the Deep South." *Journal of Poverty Research* 11: 55–81.

Hill-Collins, Patricia. 1994. "Shifting the Center: Race, Class, and Feminist Theorizing About Motherhood" in *Mothering: ideology, experience, and agency.* Ed. Glenn and Chang. New York: Routledge. Pp. 45–66.

Jefferson, Thomas. 1787. *Notes on Virginia.* in Merrill D. Peterson, *Writings of Thomas Jefferson* (New York: The Library of America, 1984) Pp. 264–66, 270.

Johnson, James Hugo. 1970. *Race Relations in Virginia & Miscegenation in the South, 1776–1860.* Mass: University of Massachusetts Press. Kennedy, Randall. 2003. Interracial Intimacies: Sex, Marriage, Identity and Adoption. New York: Pantheon Books.

Lewis, Neil. 2007. "Justice Secures His Place as a Critic of Integration " in *New York Times.* New York City.

Logan, John, Zhang Wenquan and Richard D. Alba. 2002. "Immigrant Enclaves and Ethnic Communities in New York and Los Angeles." American Sociological Review 67:299–322.

Mauro, Tony. 2007. "Thomas Recusal Mystery Solved." *BLT: The Blog of Legal Times* http://legaltimes.typepad.com/blt/2007/04/recusal_mystery.html.

Merida, Kevin and Michael Fletcher. 2007. *Supreme Discomfort: The Divided Soul of Clarence Thomas.* New York: Doubleday.

Mount Vernon. Nd. *The Mount Vernon Collections.* http://www.mountvernon.org/learn/collections/index.cfm/.

Merton, Robert. 1948. "Discrimination and the American Creed." Pp. 99–126. *Discrimination and National Welfare* (ed.) R.M. MacIver. New York: Harper and Brothers.

Noonan, Peggy. 1997. "Looking Forward." *Good Housekeeping.* February 1, 1997.

Omi, Michael and Howard Winant. 1989. *Racial Formation in the United States: From the 1960s to the 1980s.* New York: Routledge.

Okoye , F. Nwabueze. 1980. Chattel Slavery as the Nightmare of the American Revolutionaries. *The William and Mary Quarterly.* Third Series. 37(1): 4–28.

Parks, Robert. 1973. "The Development of Segregation in US Army Hospitals, 1940–1942." *Military Affairs* 37: 145–150.

Patterson, Orlando. 1999. *Rituals of Blood: Consequences of Slavery in Two American Centuries*. New York: Civitas.

Pompeian, Ed. 2005. "George Washington Slave Child." *History News Network*: George Mason University, March 31.

Qian, Zhenchao and Daniel Lichter. 2007. "Social Boundaries and Marital Assimilation: Interpreting Trends in Racial and Ethnic Intermarriage." *American Sociological Review* 72: 68–94.

Rayner, B.L. 1834. *Thomas Jefferson*. Boston: Lilly, Wait, Colman, & Holden. Available at: The University of Virginia Archives. http://etext.virginia.edu/jefferson/biog/. Accessed November 4, 2008.

Rivkin, David and Lee Casey. 2008. "Clarence Thomas Mr. Constitution." P. A25 in *Wall Street Journal*. New York.

Rollins, Judith. 1985. *Between Women: Domestics and Their Employers*. Philadelphia, PA: Temple University Press.

Segura, Denise A. 1994 "Working at Motherhood: Chicana and Mexican Immigrant Mothers and Employment." In *Mothering: Ideology, Experience, and Agency*. Eds: Glenn and Chang. New York: Routledge. Pp. 211–236.

Senate, United States. n.d. http://www.senate.gov/artandhistory/history/common/generic/VP_Richard_M_Johnson.htm.

Soskis, Benjamin. Nd. "Heroic Exile: The Transatlantic Development of Frederick Douglass, 1845–1847." Gilder Lehrman Center for the study of Slavery, Resistance, and Abolition. New Haven Connecticut, Yale University. http://www.yale.edu/glc/soskis/pt5.htm.

Staples, Brent. 2008. Loving v. Virginia and the Secret History of Race. *New York* Times. May 14. Staples, Brent. 2008. Savoring the Undertones and Lingering Subtleties of Obama's Victory Speech. *New York Times*. November 8.

Staples, Brent. 2003. Editorial Observer; Senator Strom Thurmond's Deception Ravaged Two Lives. *New York Times*. December 26.

Stearns, Linda Brewester and John Logan. 1986. "The Racial Structuring of the Housing Market in Suburban Areas." *Social Forces* 65: 128–142.

Stritof, Bob, Sheri. "Mildred Jeter and Richard Loving Marriage Profile." 9 Nov 2008. http://marriage.about.com/od/historical/p/lovingjeter.htm.

Taylor, Michael. 2007. PROFILES: Sally Hemings. *Richmond Times-Dispatch*. November 11, 2007. Accessed online http://www.inrich.com/cva/ric/news/blackhistory.apx.-content-articles-RTD-special-0541.html. November 8, 2008.

TerBeek, Calvin J., 2006. "Write Separately: Justice Clarence Thomas's 'Race Opinions' on the Supreme Court." *Texas Journal on Civil Liberties & Civil Rights* 11: 185–210.

Therborn, Göran. 1980. *The Ideology of Power and the Power of Ideology*. London: Verso.

Thomas, Andrew Peyton. 2002. *Clarence Thomas: A Biography*. New York: Encounter Books.

Thomas, Clarence. 2007. *My Grandfather's Son: A Memoir*. New York: Harper.

Thomas Jefferson Encyclopedia. http://wiki.monticello.org/media wiki/index.php/Jefferson%27s_Formal_Education. Accessed November 4, 2008.

Thomas Jefferson Foundation: Thomas Jefferson Monticello. http://www.monticello.org/index.html. Accessed: November 5, 2008.

Twohig, Dorothy. 2001. "That Species of Property: Washington's Role in the Controversy over Slavery." *George Washington Reconsidered*. (ed.) D. Higgbotham. Charlottesville, VA: University of Virginia Press.

Walker, Dionne. "Pioneer of interracial marriage looks back." 10 Jun 2007. http://www.usatoday.com/news/nation/2007-06-10-loving_N.htm.

Washington-Williams, Essie Mae and William Stadiem. 2005. *Dear Senator: A Memoir by the Daughter of Strom Thurmond*. New York: Regan Books.

Welna, David. 2002. "Strom Thurmond: Colorful South Carolinian, Oldest Living U.S. Senator." National Public Radio (NPR). Accessed on line: November 12, 2008. http://www.npr.org/templates/story/story.php?storyId=865900.

White House Biographies. 2008. Accessed November 5. http://www.whitehouse.gov/history/firstladies/mj3.html.

Williams, Lena. 1986. "Equal Employment Official Wins Approval For 2d Term." in *New York Times*.

Williamson, Joel. (1980/1995). *New People: Miscegenation and Mulattoes in the United States*. Baton Rouge, LA: Louisiana State University Press.

Wyatt-Brown, Bertram. 1982. *Southern Honor: Ethics and Behavior in the Old South*. New York: Oxford University Press

Index